To: Carolyn Clark
We can live in
Harmony!

Bill Reely
Thank You!

MW00887750

THE GIFT OF CRITICISM

Making the Most of Critical Communication

BILL NEELY

WESTBOW
PRESS°
A DIVISION OF THOMAS NELSON
& ZONDERVAN

WestBow Press books may be ordered through booksellers or by contacting:

WestBow Press
A Division of Thomas Nelson & Zondervan
1663 Liberty Drive
Bloomington, IN 47403
www.westbowpress.com
1 (866) 928-1240

ISBN: 978-1-5127-9139-6 (sc)
ISBN: 978-1-5127-9138-9 (hc)
ISBN: 978-1-5127-9140-2 (e)

Library of Congress Control Number: 2017909965

Print information available on the last page.

WestBow Press rev. date: 7/19/2017

Contents

Foreword

Sometimes a book is written that brings such potential for healing and health that it surprises the reader to the core. This book is one of them. There are at least three things that will happen to you as you read this writing.

First, you will learn a language that will describe the trouble you may have around conflict that will bring new insights and knowledge. In this book you will gain insights that will guide you for years to come through many situations where conflict may show up. You will have a new vocabulary (knowledge) that will allow you to move past the emotional response to a reasonable approach to conflict issues.

Second, there's something very special here around the excitement that I gained, excitement of wanting to learn about relationships and what can keep them healthy. I do not recall of ever having that happen to me in dealing with the subject of conflict and resolution. To put it in the vernacular, it turned me on to want to learn more. So, this book, if it is the first one you have read in the area of conflict will most likely motivate you to keep reading in the area of intense interaction between individuals and groups. Not many books do that but this one does.

Third, this book is very pragmatic. Meaning it introduces you to skills and behaviors that you can adapt for you own life and bring you a sense of competency in managing your own emotions and behavior during a time of conflict.

John S. Savage, DMin
Conflict manager, author, trainer

Endorsements

Most people never learn how to criticize effectively or receive criticism. *The Gift of Criticism* is a great and timely book. Generally, we fall into reflexive patterns that we have seen or endured. Like lions or skunks, we roar to intimidate, or project odious invectives to disable the confidence of those whom we fear may hurt us. This book is a primer in how to give and receive criticism so that relationships and personalities are not injured.

Bill Neely, husband, father, engineer, pastor, chaplain, coach, and my friend, mentored me when I was a young pastoral aspirant. His situational awareness, listening skills, fogging technique, and sterling integrity have calibrated and guided my interactions for years. I read the book and took copious notes. Just as I did, the reader will experience aha moments in every chapter. The exercises detailed will be the catalysts of breakthroughs and springboards to inner peace from which healthy and wholesome interactions will flow.

The Gift of Criticism is definitive and expansive. Used well, it can bridge troubled waters and soothe wounded spirits. It should be required reading for everyone who is interested in fostering good relationships. Employers, spouses, educators, and leaders in any discipline or industry will be benefitted by the wisdom born of Bill's experience and research.

Paul S. Anderson, DMin
CDR, CHC, USN
Deputy chaplain
JFHQ-NCR

****

Using examples from his personal life and experiences as a chaplain and counselor, Bill Neely examines the role that criticism plays in every relationship we have. He offers practical suggestions on how to use criticism to strengthen and improve our connections with one another and on how we can receive criticism as a gift from those we care about. This is a wise and insightful book that I will read often.

Suzanne Carbone
Former librarian, Montgomery County (Maryland) Public Libraries

****

The Gift of Criticism delivers practical and useful techniques to effectively deal with a topic that's a challenge for most people. From a committed author who desires to make a difference in the world, one person at a time, this message is truly a gift to be absorbed and appreciated.

Nancy Oscheinreiter
Healthcare volunteer coordinator
CCRC

****

In his book, my friend Bill presents a fresh and eye-opening perspective on criticism. It is informative, instructive, and written in a relatable way. All of us, individuals, groups, and nations, can benefit from the lessons that are taught here. We each receive criticism. How do we handle it?

For iron to sharpen iron, the contact is abrasive, but when handled properly, the knife is sharpened. So, too, in the interface of human relationships, criticism (well-intended or not) can sometimes be abrasive. The recipient can use this as a stepping stone to sharpen his knife so that he may reach the grapes that are higher on the vine, or it may become to him a stumbling block, piercing the ego of his soul and limiting his access to the richness of the vine. It all depends on how the recipient chooses to respond.

Bill has expertly placed the conversation before us with an abundance of relatable experiences. The lessons are universal and present practical ideas and solutions to transform your thoughts, presentations and response to receiving criticism.

This book has the power to change all of us for the better. I commend it to you.

Oscar L. Avant
Inventor, pastor, author
Silver Spring, Maryland

****

When first reading this book, I was intrigued with the concept of criticism being a gift. Its examples provide a clear and practical guide to approaching difficult behavioral matters in personal and business relationships. So often there is reluctance to address real-life issues for fear of offending or hurting another's feelings. This book offers candid advice and spot-on solutions. It is refreshing to read and remains with you long after you finish it. It is about honesty and truthfulness in the truest sense. All friends, family, employees, and business leaders alike deserve access to William Neely's *The Gift of Criticism*.

Melanie Rankin, PHR
Human resources manager
The Salvation Army, National Capital Area Command
Washington, DC

****

Bill Neely offers us insights into how to correct ourselves and communicate more effectively by paying closer attention to what matters most: how we treat others. It's not about us, rather how we treat others with our words, actions, and expressions. This is a read, reread, and valuable reference book.

Tony Ruesing, CSP
Author and director of training
Faithful Brain Institute

****

Bill Neely's book, *The Gift of Criticism*, offers a unique perspective in its view of offering and receiving criticism in all spheres of our lives (personal, professional, familial). This book is useful for readers of all professions, backgrounds, cultures—anyone who is interested in improving his or her communication skills, self-awareness, and ability to respond to criticism in a productive way while also offering criticism in a tactful and respectful manner.

Bill, a colleague of mine, personally exemplifies a masterful use of offering and receiving criticism in the workplace. He has earned the respect, admiration, and appreciation from me as well as many at our organization. In sharing his own personal life experiences, Bill also exemplifies how one's history impacts our ability to receive and offer criticism. *The Gift of Criticism* is an inspiring, motivating book that challenges us all to seek out the biggest room—the room for improvement.

Wisma Satriano, LCSW-C
Licensed clinical social worker

****

A gift, indeed!

In this new book, Bill Neely has launched a paradigm shift that could transform the ways in which criticism is conceptualized, proffered, received, and internalized. His deft reframing of this often-maligned construct has the potential to improve communications in families, faith communities, workplaces, and countless other venues where human beings interact with one another. My hope is that readers will use this powerful gift to effect positive changes in their lives and in the lives of those they love.

Barbara H. Suddarth, PhD
Psychologist and organizational consultant

****

Testimonial

If I were writing a list of people who *contributed* to my *life*, you'd be up there! Just think of you when I hear, see, or read anything about criticism, as you've forever changed my personal meaning of the word.

Brenda Norris
ACC, AC-BC

Introduction

There's a broad arena of critics in literature, art, music, entertainment, science, history, food, sports, politics, finance, war, theater, and more. *Critics* in these and other areas are sought out for their views, expertise, and opinions. For many, being a critic is an occupation, and some make of it a career. Coaches criticize aspects of the players' games and lives, and they can become champions. Orchestra conductors critique musicians about that single score, chord, or note that makes "all the difference in the world." These individuals and groups seek continual improvement; they expect, accept, and welcome criticism as an essential element of their improvement. Many will receive the coveted designation—critically acclaimed!

There's a multitude of critics in the greater public society comprised of parents, siblings, teachers, students, bosses, coworkers, leaders, coaches, athletes, and a plethora of others who criticize based on their perceptions of what is, isn't, should, or should not be. Their basis for being critical and criticizing may rest largely on a limited view or perspective of life centering around their experiences, inheritances, and opinions, expressing disapproval of someone or something as faults and mistakes. This contrasts with the more professional critics cited in the previous paragraph.

In this book criticism is regarded as an evaluation instrument or tool intended to improve or advance relationships, experiences, and understanding in all areas of life with the goal of having mutually beneficial outcomes for all involved parties. This definition is expanded to include complaints, perceptions, beliefs, observations, and opinions. This book sees the best of criticism, and presents criticism at its best by regarding it as an intention to improve or advance a situation or relationship. The anticipated outcome is positive. I also look at this as Criticism 2.0

> To avoid criticism, say nothing, do nothing, be nothing.
> —Aristotle

Criticism is a powerful communication tool that can yield benefits to enhance, enrich, and improve life when skillfully executed. If done poorly, criticism can wreak havoc.

Here you will discover pointers on how to present, receive, and respond to criticism, whether at home, at work, in school, and in other places and settings. You'll learn how to lighten burdens and reduce *friction* often associated with presenting or responding to complaints and criticism, as well as lessen the strain and tension in relationships. You may be astonished or at least pleasantly surprised at how you can address and resolve tension, heal, and improve relationships through the skillful presentation and reception of criticism. Other instances may call for more time, energy, and creativity to reach a mutually beneficial outcome. And yes, there are likely to be some special instances where one or both parties decide to leave things as they are and walk away without any physical harm, with that being a type of mutually beneficial outcome. Energy, skill, focus, openness, and intention are crucial in determining whether an experience will be simple and easy, complex, or difficult—depending on the level and degree of honesty, reliability, expectations, and ego issues.

The desired goal and objective in using the tools of criticism in this book is to establish, build, and maintain harmony in relationships, and to have mutually beneficial outcomes. The concepts shared herein have universal application for personal or individual use and for family, organizational, and social settings as well as the community and nation. They apply in every discipline. The long-range goal is to transition toward a cooperative world, where we all can live, work, study, play, explore, design, and create environments that foster cooperation and appreciation rather than the festering competition that divides, demeans, and often destroys. In light of all that has been accomplished through ingenuity, genius, steadfastness, determination, and cooperation on a limited basis, I am satisfied that we have the capacity and capability to foster healthy and wholesome relationships among the members of our human families.

My understanding of criticism was transformed in 1983, in a workshop entitled "Learning the Language of Healing," presented by Dr. John Savage, founder of LEAD Consultants, Inc., who wrote the preface for this book. This was my introduction to the universal nature and power of communication and its essential role in forming, building, and shaping healthy or not so healthy intra- and interpersonal relationships.

Dr. Savage's workshop was a dramatic awakening and a life-altering experience that challenged and inspired me to study, learn, focus on. and practice communication skills (beyond the basics of reading, writing. and talking) that had previously eluded me in life experiences, education, and training. Otherwise, it is likely that I could have dismissed as irrelevant any information about relationships during my college years and the ten years in my engineering career.

At age thirty-seven, I had this rich, practical learning experience that focused on enhanced listening (which is akin to reading the fine print) and being intentional in communicating—especially with criticism. I learned methods of extinguishing or lowering the intensity of potentially explosive situations, dramatically reducing tension and friction, thus improving communication and relationships. This even applied to my relationship with myself.

The course of my life was altered in ways that I never imagined, beginning with my attitude and behavior about presenting, receiving, and responding to criticism. There was a change from avoidance and denial to acknowledgment, acceptance, and eventually appreciation of criticism— even the uncomfortable aspects. I became less fretful about making a mistake, having made a mistake in the past, or failing at something. Mistakes can be portals to accomplishment and achievement for life experiences, by design or serendipity, that may not be realized devoid of them. Shifting my communication skills eventually led to a shift in my outlook on life, which lead me to the healing of strained childhood memories, experiences, and relationships.

This turn of events enabled me to reflect on and observe communication patterns and practices among people. Some of these patterns and practices were routine, even predictable. There were pitfalls and potholes that contributed to the breakdown of relationships in the form of arguments, fights, name-calling, resentment, and falling out among family members, congregants, coworkers, and colleagues that sometimes resulted in sustained negativity. There were patterns and practices that resulted in understanding (which for me means objective information; unbiased facts; acknowledgment of temperament, culture, context, style, generation; sensory recognition with emotional links to what the other is experiencing) at deeper levels that was often transformative.

These observations and experiences then guided me to immersion, attention to information and concepts about communication and, particularly, about criticism. Then the transformation occurred, from being curious about the role and impact of communication on relationships to being interested, to becoming passionate, to developing plans and programs that help us improve how we relate with ourselves, each other in the home, school, church, and community. Similar plans and programs by a plethora of other like-minded individuals are relevant across the spectrum of people on the planet.

As a concept, I think of a world where many of the commonplace attitudes and actions of disharmony, oppression, and violence will be as unusual, astonishing, and outdated as manual typewriters, computer punch cards, or travel by Conestoga wagon. Attitudes and behaviors such as name-calling, teasing, vulgarity, bullying, stereotyping, domestic violence, rage, fighting, and war would be recorded in history books and housed in archives telling stories of the way life used to be.

I see us immersed in a laboratory of human-relationship experiences and experiments throughout the span and spectrum of history and imagination. Some seek to compete, conquer, and dominate. Some are actively seeking to live cooperatively. Many comfortably abide in past-oriented mind-sets, justifying the way things are based on the way things have always been (the inheritance factor), refusing to lend support toward broad relationship improvements. Others are deeply immersed in an awareness of and acknowledging our unavoidable interdependence and mutual need for each other; and they are working toward a cooperative (versus competitive) model for the future that will result in more of us living together in harmony. Doing so will help us become more fully human, learning from failed experiments of mayhem and greed that have littered the planet with bloodshed and untold horrific tragedies. The reasons or excuses for why we have failed to do better are legion. Fear, lies, comfort, and the herd mentality are among the explanations that cause many to readily embrace flawed psychosocial traditions and beliefs that feed perceptions of unavoidable mutual enmity. Excusing human behavior as human nature is another factor in the search for justification of the status quo and dismissing the greater possibilities for a different world.

We seem to prefer functioning based on demographic and socioeconomic basis such as occupation, zip code, profession, income, class, social rating, and other categories, rather than building cross-spectrum relationships designed and established to enhance our living together as fellow humans sharing the same air.

As a collective, we generally support changes and upgrades for *things* that are used by people, insisting that these things be designed and developed with care and safety concerns. There are reviews and critiques of the design and plans, followed by inspections, permits, testing, licenses, instructions or directions for use, and the like to provide levels of oversight, responsibility, and accountability to ensure safety, comfort, and sales for the future while minimizing the possibilities of lawsuits. The current massive and powerful consumeristic view and concept of people as marketing and sales data and resources fosters the frenzy of a competitive culture steeped in buying and selling for profit or gain as a primary goal or objective. Yet the notion of upgrading our communication and relationship skills to promote and enhance cooperative living as fellow humans is often met with instant rejection, dismissed as an impossible dream or the musings of those who have nothing useful to offer for living in the "real world."

Reflective interlude

As I ponder some of what humans in the real world have achieved over millennia in the realms of science, technology, communications, travel, agriculture, medicine, transportation, geology, trade, genetics, and energy, to name merely a few, and the numerous benefits that accompanied these achievements to benefit individuals, families, communities, and the world, it seems clear to me that we can include harmonious living as an achievable goal. These triumphs and associated side effects happened because of the human ability, willingness, and risk to communicate and connect with other humans of different cultures and class. It is notable that some people who work together cooperatively on the job to improve and upgrade products and services refuse to be cooperative beyond the defined/inherited socio-graphics with the same coworkers beyond the workplace.

Based on what has been done in the areas cited above and so much more, it is within the realm of possibility that we can communicate in ways that promote relationship understanding, cooperation, and harmony across the spectrum and amid the diverse tapestry of humanity.

I see the possibility of us shifting the elements of our mutual existence toward congruity in various ways, honing our communication skills and arriving at clearer understanding, mutual appreciation, and interdependence.

Imagine that we decide to express equal or greater care and concern for the relationships between and among people, to ensure and enhance mutual respect and appreciation for people. Imagine that we have the same or greater care for relationships as we do for products. Imagine business owners, coworkers, parents, and teachers placing equal or higher value, care, and concern for the people they interact with as they do for the products and services that will be used by people. This can begin by incorporating specific communication skills related to criticism into the training and education programs everywhere—starting at home and infusing the community, schools, universities, workplaces, religious and political realms.

Learning and implementing skilled presentation of and response to criticism will improve the attitude and manner of the criticism in all areas of life and help us move toward living in harmony.

Imagine improving your relationships (including that crucial foundational relationship with yourself) by improving your skills in the realm of criticism. Alterations in concept, attitude, belief and practices will bring this improvement into existence. Proverb 23:7 rings quite true in this regard.

> As we think in our hearts so are we (or) so we become.
> —KJV

This holds true for criticism as well as other aspects of life.

Exercise

Let's check this out with a brief exercise. Get a pen and paper and prepare to write down your first thoughts and impressions in a few moments. Put the date on your paper. Secure a quiet place and empty your hands and your lap. Take a few deep breaths.

Remember to breathe correctly—stomach goes out as you inhale. This intentional act is essential to better manage stress. Improper breathing is a source of added stress. Close your eyes and relax for a minute.

Now continue the exercise.

When you hear or see the word *criticism*, write down the words, thoughts, images, pictures, feelings, or sounds that come to mind. Give yourself time to reflect. Breathe! After exhausting your thoughts on the topic, let's see the power and truth of the proverb.

- Your thoughts about criticism determine your feelings about criticism.

- These feelings generate an attitude.
- This attitude determines your behavioral response to criticism.
- Your behavior establishes a habit pattern.
- This habit pattern sets your character in place.
- Your character ultimately determines your destiny.

The tendency for most people is to say that criticism is negative with a fight-or-flight outcome as the instinctive default. As they think, they will act to make the thoughts so. This book offers information, and that can shift the thinking about criticism so people can act differently and make the world different.

Please turn to Pages 129 and 130 and take the survey that 130 people filled out. Demographic information is in the appendix. Take the survey now and then take it after reading the book. Please share your experience and any changes with me at bill@gettingalongbetterllc.com.

I have diagramed the proverb using the following diagram that was illustrated by my daughter Nicole.

Nicole illustrated the cover and all diagrams in this book.

Note: This diagram is designed by Nicole

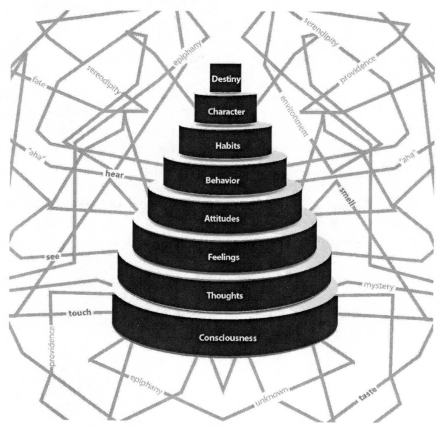

Proverbs 23:7: "As we think in our hearts, so we become."

While the diagram shows the steps or process of moving from thoughts to destiny, please notice the maze of lines in the background. These represent elements of influence beyond our awareness or consciousness and the mystery of the divine, or the unknown, that may impact us on our journeys.

End of exercise

Our greater potential as humans living in harmony has gone largely untapped as a massive universal body of humankind. The potential I speak of resides mostly dormant in our abilities to communicate across the human spectrum—as has been noted above. This means we have the ability and capability to communicate within and among all the people (cross spectrum) of the planet in a cooperative manner. I think of all of us as members of the massive body of humankind, with diverse parts that provide specific functions to contribute to the betterment of all members of the body. We are more than categories of class, status, nationality, color, or ethnicity. We are more than census data or other categories plotted on the bell curve or other related charts. Are you comfortable being referenced as a resource, product, human capital or collateral damage? Such labeling and categorization contributes to the undermining and sabotaging of our broader relationship potential.

We are greater than the sum of our groups, numbers, and the like.

I see the potential and possibility for building relationships that support and foster interdependence, appreciation, mutual respect, and love. Such relationships can be mutually beneficial in financial matters, perhaps more so than the brutal commerce-centered approach that operates currently.

Genuine security occurs when there is trust, mutual respect, mutual protection, and benefit as we gaze upon each other with eyes that enable us to see ourselves in each other. Experiments are welcome. The lab is always open!

End of interlude

I see upgrades in relationships as a possibility just as there are upgrades in science, technology, transportation, and myriad other areas of life. I do understand the challenge.

We readily expect and accept technical upgrades and gladly pay for them, while eagerly awaiting (if not demanding) the next upgrade. In the same way, each day can be an opportunity to practice and affirm the benefits of listening, learning, changing, and improving relationships. These practices are as vital to our individual and societal well-being as the regular, consistent training and development that is expected in the areas of athletics, academics, entertainment, research, medicine, and business.

Fans, franchise owners, teammates, advertisers and opponents expect, even demand improvements. Universities and corporations constantly seek and thrive on advancements. Even tire companies are perpetually reinventing the wheel. These achievements and accomplishments are a source of inspiration that can propel people to reach higher, stretch further, and live better than they previously thought possible.

This book is an offering of skills to apply in the realm of criticism as a contribution toward us living in harmony among the people on the planet.

My hope is to provide tools that will be used to reframe criticism and transform your relationships in a positive revolutionary way. You'll learn to embrace and capitalize upon the benefits of criticism leading to specific intentional communication that satisfies the critic and brings benefit to the *critizen* (a new term that is explained below). This attitude and approach promotes the garnering of insight, courage, and skill in presenting, seeking, receiving, and responding to criticism. By learning these principles and applying the skills, we can advance our relationships in the direction of greater harmony and less discord. Criticism can be mutually beneficial, not merely a matter of right and wrong with the concomitant result of yielding a winner and a loser.

Additionally, readers will learn proactive ways to seek criticism prior to taking a specific action. People can partner with each other and others, and share thoughts and information that could be helpful in shaping the way a matter is approached, thus minimizing or avoiding damage in specific situations. For example, some musicians say to each other in rehearsals, "Please tell me when I make a mistake or where I can improve." By inviting or seeking criticism in advance, they foster a mutual agreement, build trust, and establish harmony among the band members resulting in a better performance by the band. The presupposition is cooperative, not competitive. No gloating, finger-pointing, gossiping, backbiting, or splitting. Each is better and everyone benefits from their mutual critiques. It's a gift!

Let's apply the aspects of criticism that makes for better athletes, welders, carpenters, masons, and the like to all our relationships. Let's make criticism a gift in all areas of life.

Throughout this book, I will be using three terms related to criticism. One, you are familiar with—the critic (the focus is on improvement and mutual benefits). The other two are words I have coined. The *critizen* is the person being criticized. The *critizone* comprises the pertinent elements associated with a specific criticism, such as the relationship between the critic and critizen, the nature of the criticism (constructive, mutually beneficial, urgent, etc.), setting, time and the like.

Adding these two words to the realm of criticism will aid in reducing much of the negative attitude and feelings about criticism. The bad reputation of criticism has led many to regularly, routinely avoid, deny, or excuse problems that need to be addressed at home, work, school, and in the community. Unwittingly letting known problems go unattended, incubating for lengthy periods, often contributes to an eventual eruption and even great harm.

Expanding the meaning and experience of criticism 1.0 beyond the limits of disapproval, faults, and mistakes that focused either on the critic or the citizen to a focus on both learning and becoming skilled brings a more balanced approach and more positive feelings among affected parties who will know that the citizen and the critizone, along with the critic, are involved in shaping, influencing, and directing the outcome of the experience.

The critic who raises an issue along with the citizen know that either or both can alter the experience and the outcome as both make the best use of the numerous elements of the critizone. The context of a situation alters the experience. For example, change will occur in an experience if it is indoors or outdoors, lighting, sound, a sunny or overcast sky, loud or soft music, a smile or a frown, food present or not. The critic or the citizen or both can move the experience toward or away from harmony. Either can shift to dancing or to fighting.

Since everyone will be in the role of critic and citizen as life unfolds, it is beneficial for all to understand that criticism can enhance the quality of life.

With the concepts and skills presented in this book I hope to raise the awareness of seeking options beyond the win/lose, fight/flight/freeze default positions. I invite you to lend your support to an improved way of life by learning and implementing improved skills and attitudes regarding criticism.

The lab is always open!

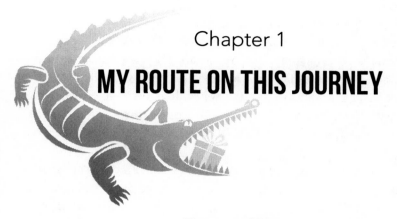

Chapter 1

MY ROUTE ON THIS JOURNEY

Unexpected Favors

During an early morning bicycle ride in 2008, the following thought came to me as clear as the Liberty Bell.

The person who criticizes me is doing me a favor (offering a gift!).

This thought was a bit disquieting, and it lingered, leading me to review and ponder some significant, past personal, hurtful, embarrassing, harsh, even crude criticisms. Sometimes without conscious awareness, memories of these experiences had accompanied me on the journey of life for decades after they had happened. As I struggled with the thought of the critic doing me a favor, the insight came when I recognized and acknowledged the truth of the criticism and the corresponding changes I'd made that had improved that aspect of my life. Many criticisms had indeed been favors. I'd learned and benefitted from them, and I'd eventually come to regard them as gifts—unexpected for sure, yet still gifts. Because of that bike ride on that day, I reassessed and redefined those aspects of my past that resulted in a paradigm shift that acknowledges that criticism could be beneficial. A few months later, I began presenting seminars and workshops on the topic of criticism as a gift, and that eventually led to the writing of this book.

Here are a few of the more significant criticisms from my past that were examined and altered. At the times described, I regarded criticism as bad or negative, and I did what I could to avoid or deny it until the lessons and benefits were manifested to me.

Childhood

My earliest memories of childhood were flooded with statements of disapproval, expressed as criticism, complaints, and perceived expressions of displeasure. My mom, relatives, the community, some teachers, and others trained me (and children in general) to be quiet and compliant, never complaining or questioning the way things were. Accept, absorb, or "deal" with the harsh realities of life. One of the cardinal rules of the community regarding children was, "Children should be seen and not heard."

I sensed that I was immersed in a turbulent ocean awash with waves of negative and critical statements that ebbed and flowed over me. I generally felt unfit and confused about life. At times, it seemed I was all alone with no one to talk to or discuss the questions, observations, and concerns that I had.

My father was my life raft and protector until he died when I was six years old. From that time through high school, college, and into young adult life, I followed the social order when it came to criticism. Stifle, defend, excuse, retaliate in kind, deny, justify, or find some scapegoat as a response to a criticism. And when it came to presenting criticism, oh well. Be tough, thick skinned, crude, cruel, and uncaring. Trade insults, resort to name-calling, and by all means, win the argument or contest. When a crowd is present, make sure they think you got the best of the other person. After the encounter, put energy into preparing for the next time, because whoever "lost" had to get back at the winner or at least get even. So, there was going to be another event. On and on it went until at last one succumbed, yielded, gave up with various accompanying labels, walked away as a loser, or got in serious trouble with a family in the community or the law as result of getting even and wanting to win.

These are a few of the criticisms that proved to be gifts presented by people with different personalities, methods, styles and approaches. Some were easier to bear than others. Most of these gifts were presented with the intent to be hurtful or humiliating or to shame me in some way, or at least to get their voice heard above mine. I carried this concept for decades. Then along came another idea that these were gifts that benefitted me.

Body Odor—High School

I think back to a rather crude criticism presented to me by a teammate on the high school basketball team. As I left the game, coming to the bench, he said, "You need to wash yourself; you stink." It was loud enough for others to hear. I was embarrassed and felt humiliated. I wanted to disappear so no one would know that I was the critizen. There was slight refuge that, in an athletic contest, the critizone with all the physical exertion, there could be an expectation of some degree of body odor. It would likely have been less embarrassing if this had happened in the locker room and not in the gym during the game. Nonetheless, that was a paradigm-shift experience. I benefitted by attending to my hygiene every day. I changed—due to the criticism, complaint, or observation—and implemented the lesson of soap, water, and deodorant so that criticism has never been directed at me since. As it turns out, I am grateful that the teammate spoke up. Lesson learned with no expiration date. Extended shelf life!

Had that matter been avoided or excused, who knows how long it might have taken before I would be mortified in a more awkward setting or situation? I would likely have heard similar iterations and perhaps become the talk of the team or the school in regard to poor hygiene. I might have become so ashamed as to feel the need to defend myself, fight, or find some fault with him, hurt or embarrass him, or just quit the team. If I had decided to get even, I would be certain of getting into a fight with him and his posse. That could have resulted in my being hurt or me hurting him. I could have been kicked off the team and had to watch my back for the rest of the season or school year, or I could have been suspended from school. If I were kicked out of school, then I would have been confronted by my mother. Oh, me! That would have been the worst thing that could happen. Fortunately, the embarrassment went a long way to making my life better, hygienically speaking. Though embarrassing at the time, I received a great gift.

I cited several what-ifs above, because lots of people act defensively and find reasons to fight back or get even rather than examining the criticism, learning, and applying the appropriate lessons.

Not heeding the lesson(s) of criticism generally brings about repeated messages making their bid for acceptance and implementation. It's like a delivery person bringing a package to your home repeatedly because no one is there to receive it. In the case of criticism, if the package (lesson of the message) is not received, multiple individuals will repeatedly attempt the delivery. There is no warning that says if the package (criticism) is not received after three attempts it will be returned to the sender. No!

Numerous "delivery people" will leave notes at the door, perhaps from different companies and in different uniforms, indefinitely. For those who tend to get the message and the lesson in the first or second attempt, receive the message, learn from it, and implement the lesson, the delivery person no longer stops by to leave a note for that package (criticism).

Criticism can be a small price to pay for improvements that result in correction or success. What a gift, especially when presented by a friend or a family member who genuinely cares and displays courage, tact, and skill in their presentation of a criticism.

Yet many times those in close relationships unwittingly defer, enabling if not empowering the troubling behavior, leaving it to fester, waiting for or hoping that someone else will be the agent (delivery person) to point out the need for change and correction. This is an expression of the bystander effect, when an individual or a group of people think, believe, or rely on someone else to act. The larger the number of observers or bystanders, the more likely the group thinks or believes that someone else will act yet not do so.

Many people avoid presenting a criticism due to the fears of hurting someone's feelings, getting someone in trouble, retribution, or harming a relationship, or just not wanting to be involved. Unfounded or neurotic rationalizations about giving criticism can be a source of anxiety that limits or prevents an individual or group from addressing a matter. When someone is hurt due to a criticism, sometimes the critic can immerse himself or herself in self-blame for lengthy periods of time (extended shelf life), regretting his or her action or failing to make amends for the criticism. It could be a parent, teacher, friend, or coworker.

Take the example of halitosis. Someone in your family, a friend, coworker, or choir member has bad breath. What do you do? Do you tell the person by *talking to* him or her? Or do you *talk about* the person to all the other people you know? Do you hesitate and think of all the reasons you shouldn't tell the person who has the problem? What will they think of me if I tell them? What will they think of me when they find out I told everyone else? Will they dislike me or point out some problem I have? Will I pick a time and place that will be the least embarrassing or just let it out in the most humiliating setting with witnesses?

If someone outside that close circle of family, coworkers, or choir offers the criticism and the citizen inquires of those in the close circle regarding the matter, there may be an acknowledgment of fear or reluctance to criticize, to the dismay of the citizen. The citizen may express disappointment or anger that others merely stood by and watched as the problem grew. Or the citizen may have previously expressed anger at someone in the close circle who treaded on that very delicate ground to make the matter known, thus warding off others.

I'll share some concepts and principles that can be easily adapted and applied to situations like this.

As the citizen, there may be some degree of discomfort. Hopefully, it will be minimal and come to be regarded as beneficial, even if it was beyond minimal discomfort. The truth is, the critic or coach *usually* has some insight or information to share that could possibly be beneficial to themselves or the citizen and maybe both. The teacher or coach guides, directs, and criticizes the student or athlete toward better. The journeyman or mentor does the same for an apprentice or mentee. Rarely will a coach feel guilty because of criticizing a player who eventually becomes a star. Some coaches yell and scream at the players. Others have specific ways of addressing the individual, team, or group based on the peculiarities of the situation. The way the criticism is presented has shelf life and proves to have an impact on the coach and the student.

Hurt feelings on the part of the citizen can be acknowledged and expressed in some situations. In other situations, it may be better to express such feelings in a very selective setting that fosters healing and support (critizone), because some critics or coaches will add insult to the injury. There may even be a situation where the citizen may opt to avoid responding.

For instance, a player who has progressed greatly, comes to tell the coach that he didn't appreciate being yelled at on the floor. It would have been better if you had called me to the side and pointed out the problem, he might say. Some coaches may yell louder the next time and remind the playing that the yelling was what motivated him to play better and that yelling led to stardom.

This book provides insight and several ways to approach these delicate situations for mutually beneficial outcomes, using examples with specific steps to take. The reader can adapt and make modifications based on their unique situation. Awareness of options for presenting and responding using specific skills and approaches are taught to benefit parents, child care providers, coaches and teachers who can train children early in life to appreciate the benefits of correction and receiving criticism as well as how to present it and respond so there are mutually beneficial outcomes. The preferred use of criticism is to motivate and teach with the intent to improve or advance.

College

In my sophomore year of college, several "gifts" were presented to me that altered the course of my life in a positive direction. The first began with an inquiry from Albert, who lived across the hall in the dorm. He and I were in the same English class, and one day he casually asked how I did on an assignment. I showed him the paper with all the red marks. The paper was bleeding, a term referring to the extreme number of red marks the teacher had made throughout the paper. After reading the paper, Albert expressed great disappointment with punctuated expletives. "This is lousy; you can do better than this. If you need help, I'll help you. You can't turn in anything like this again." His caustic comments were embarrassing, and I would rather not have put them here.

Nonetheless, he saw that I needed help, criticized me directly and unabashedly, and offered to help me. At that point, I wasn't even sure what all was wrong with the paper, nor did I know how much help I needed. Perhaps he understood that I suffered from the Jim Crow separate-and-unequal realities of the time, or that I wasn't motivated to do my very best, or any number of reasons for turning in such a poor paper. Maybe he just saw a brother in need and, regardless of the reasons, made it a matter of personal concern, spoke up, and reached out, and I responded by facing the facts of the situation and accepting the help that was offered.

That negative experience (negative is a baseline or reference point for where one is; positive is the direction toward a destination) gave me several reasons to do better on the academic front. This became a positive experience. The English professor and Albert were the delivery people, presenting a message (criticism) of poor performance in that class. They ignited my potential. I got the message, got help, learned how to study, studied, and applied the lessons. I improved my ability to read with understanding, to write, and to critique my own writing. (This was before laptops, spell-check, and personal printers.) I made an appointment to speak with the professor to get specific assistance and directions. Albert tutored me. I resubmitted the paper and earned better grades.

For this to happen, I made several changes in my attitude and the use of time. I went to the library; spent a lot less time standing on the block, telling lies, laughing, and watching the girls go by. I stopped using the Jim Crow system as a reason not to do better now. Focused attention, intention, work, support, and understanding led to more confidence and eventually better grades. I also learned to be thankful for the criticism. It was a gift.

****

A little later in my sophomore year, while this transformation was in process, I received a notice to appear before the academic dean. This shined a bright light on my state of academic readiness. The dean was pleasant and courteous while informing me that I would be placed on academic probation, with the possibility that I might be expelled from school based on poor grades. A letter would be sent to my mother informing her of my status. He then expressed concern that college may not be right for me. Perhaps I might be better suited for a career in the service sector, mechanics, transportation, construction, or plumbing. He wasn't disparaging of these professions, but was addressing my fitness for the rigors of the academic programs.

His reasoning was based on my grades and my IQ test results. He stated that my IQ score was eighty-nine. My response was, "What's wrong with that score? It's almost an A." There was an obvious disconnect in our scales of measurement. His body language and facial expressions conveyed a sense of awe at my ignorance. It may have been that he wondered (my perception), "How did you get here in the first place?" Keep in mind that during that time period many of the HBCUs had placement tests, rather than entrance exams, that provided the opportunity for a student to possibly make up for deficits due to the Jim Crow system or other inequities.

HBCUs are historically black colleges and universities. Most of these schools were established after the American Civil War to provide academic opportunities for children of slaveholders and plantation owners born to enslaved and formerly enslaved women. These schools provided doorways for those who would otherwise be denied basic freedom as well as educational and other opportunities due to their skin color. The needs of these students would be met through remedial programs. It would then be up to the student to apply the energy and resources necessary to prove that he or she could perform on or above par with anyone else.

Since Albert had proved to be a true friend and a reliable source for academic matters, I told him about my visit with the dean. He clued me in on the differences between the academic grading scale and the IQ scale. I summarily altered my schedule even more, changed my study patterns and habits, and spent more time in the library and at my desk, reading and studying, writing papers, checking them, asking for help, and preparing for exams. I drastically reduced card playing, stopped standing out on the block altogether, and even skipped a lot of athletic events. These changes resulted in my staying in school and eventually being removed from academic probation. My redirection was an awakening of my desire to graduate from college in four years. This all came about because of what appeared to be bad news or maybe even failure by some standard. The criticism made in the form of red marks on my paper led to a redirection of my life.

****

Junior Year

During my junior year of college, this practice of study, learning, processing, synthesis, and analysis led me to challenge one of my engineering professors on the answer to an assignment. I worked the assigned problem and checked the answer in the back of the book. When I saw a different answer than I had, I reworked the problem, checked more closely, reviewed my review, and checked with a couple of other students as to their answers. No one had the answer in the back of the book and seemed unaffected. After several attempts to get the answer in the back of the book and failing to do so, I turned in the assignment with my answer, commenting that the answer in the book was wrong. The paper was returned to me with that answer marked wrong (bleeding), and a note referencing the answer in the back of the book. During class I raised my hand and expressed my position. The professor insisted that the answer in the back of the book was right and attempted to show the class how he had arrived at the answer in the book. I respectfully insisted that the method he'd used to get that answer was inconsistent with the formula. He seemed irritated that I had challenged him on this point and might have regarded it as a criticism. It may be that he was uncomfortable with the query from a student. My intent was to stay true to the formula and the equations, not merely to be right. At some point, he wanted to move on to other material.

After that class I again began working on the problem to see if I could get the answer that was in the book. After using all the tools and rules I knew, I still couldn't reconcile my answer with the answer in the book nor the professor. So, I wrote the publisher seeking a response to my dilemma. The professor moved on to other topics and problems for us to address and solve with agreement among the class on methodology and solutions. Within a week or two, the publisher answered my query, stating that the answer in the book was indeed wrong and that I had solved the problem correctly.

With this letter, I went to class, and wouldn't you know it! On that day, the first thing the professor did was to address the class about the problem that had been debated. He said to the class, "The discussion that Mr. Neely and I had about the problem and the answer in the book a week or two ago has been resolved. I am satisfied that Mr. Neely is right and that the answer in the book is wrong. So, Mr. Neely, I agree with you." I was floored and pleased, and expressed thanks to the teacher. (I have occasionally wondered if the publisher sent out a notification to the schools that the answer in the back of the book was wrong. These were pre-Internet days.) I kept my letter from the publisher in my textbook, and the class moved on to the remaining lessons. Unfortunately, that letter, book, and other items were lost when my trunk was lost or stolen during a bus trip back home.

During this experience with the professor, there were no expressions of belittling or denigrating anyone, though strong views and opinions were firmly held, and the matter was eventually resolved to the benefit of all parties, including the book publisher.

This event was a turning point, giving me a measure of confidence to take a position, substantiate it, and become competent. It instilled a measure of courage to present myself respectfully with determination based on research and application of the rules and formulas for solving problems.

Because of these critical experiences, I mustered a determination to change. I focused on the future, sought help from student counselors and tutors, and redirected my energies toward setting goals for myself. With these changes, I graduated in four years with a slightly higher than required GPA. While this is nothing to shout or write home about, in my case it did reveal that despite many negative aspects of my inheritance, a very localized concept of life, the Jim Crow experience (with its ignorance, fear, cruelty, terrorism, odious double standards, even death) and the lack of expectation for achievement beyond my local setting, I came to know that I had within me the potential to do well and even excel beyond the inherited, critical context.

As Misty Copeland says, "You can start late, look different, be uncertain, and still succeed."

The impetus to get my academic life and practice on track was ignited by several criticisms from a teammate who didn't care anything about me; by teachers; and by my friend Albert, who cared enough to be honest and share his observations, opinions, and judgments with me, rather than withholding them on a premise that I might be hurt or embarrassed. While Albert gave a criticism, he also offered and provided support. I gratefully and humbly accepted his support and experienced a life-altering paradigm shift.

> Is there someone in your life you can go to in confidence to get honest feedback and genuine support, even criticism?
>
> Are you the person someone can come to in confidence for honest, beneficial support, even if it means offering a criticism?

For the remainder of my college years, I studied, learned, pulled my grades up, and graduated. Lessons learned and applied. That message (study and ask for help) got across and has never had to be made any more regarding studying and being prepared for academic matters, as well as application to other matters.

From that time until this day, I willingly, often eagerly, spend time and energy reading, learning, noticing, exploring, questioning, growing, and hungering for more knowledge so I can expand beyond my current horizon and understanding of life in the greater world internally as well as externally. I learned from a colleague when we jointly taught adult education to former rubber plant employees who were being retrained for careers in basic electronics

The biggest room in the world is the room for improvement.

Extracurricular Criticisms

A physician whom I visited when I was around the age of twenty-eight, told me in a matter-of-fact way, "You should stop eating pork." She spoke about my ethnicity and the tendency toward compromising my health based on cultural (inherited) eating habits and traditions. I was offended, thinking, "What do you know about my culture and the context of my life situation? I am proud of my heritage. You don't understand the heritage issues of pork."

In the book *Brainwashed,* author Tom Burrell lists many reasons or excuses for continuing poor health practices, especially eating habits, on the part of many blacks in the chapter titled "Slow Suicide" (Burrell, 107–133).

After a few days of reflection and rethinking the whole matter in light of the professional competencies of the physician, I was motivated to experiment to see if I could improve my health and decided to take the advice of the person I was paying, and I stopped eating pork, though this was contrary to my inheritance and upbringing. I decided to receive the criticism/opinion delivered by that medical messenger for *my* improved health, obviating repeated messages from multiple delivery persons on the topic of pork. There are numerous messengers of health that present observations, findings, opinions and criticism to me. At times my body speaks, responding with pain or discomfort as a critique of some habit, practice, or need, in order to get my attention and so I can make changes that will enhance its functioning and my life experience.

Hypertension at times has the reputation as the silent killer. The message of this criticism may go unnoticed, unfelt, and unheard, without a measurement until something goes wrong and the body yields to the pressure. This may be repairable. There may be long-lasting, permanent damage or death. Sometimes, even with counsel, advice, and criticism, this message is ignored. I continue to modify my life practices to achieve better results and avoid as many of the accepted inherited ailments and chronic illnesses as I can.

The bathroom scales may convey messages that call attention to a need to lose or gain weight. Some people may notice the need and skirt the issue. Some people may address it and cause injury by starvation or other extreme measures. Sometimes the individual under discussion may attempt to ignore the matter by avoiding the scales only to have the message delivered by other parts of the body with a more direct announcement or call for attention. Listen and respond for beneficial outcomes as your journey continues.

Chapter 2

WARNING

Plan—Prepare—Practice

Criticism is a potent agent that possesses a duality of character as volatile and delicate as nitroglycerin: a constituent element of dynamite, rocket propellants, and other explosives; as well as a vasodilator in the treatment of angina pectoris, or chest pain felt just behind the breastbone (sternum). Nitro can take down a massive building, lift a rocket into space, or stabilize the human heart. Whenever and wherever nitro is present, safety is a prominent concern. Therefore, WARNINGS abound in the form of posters, signs, symbols, labels, and videos as well as instruction, periodic review, mandated in-service training, and other precautions for those who are involved with development, transport, storage, and use of this substance.

The intent, design, context, amount, and placement of nitro are significant factors that determine success, while ignoring or forgetting these basics can result in disaster. The dangers are so obvious that planning, preparing, and practice (scheduled and unannounced) are routine and customary in the world of nitroglycerin. Taking it for granted, ignoring, or disregarding its nature and power is unwise, costly, and can be destructive and deadly.

Beyond the warnings for nitroglycerin, there are warnings to apprise us of the dangers of plastic wrap, candles, medicines, baking soda, toothpaste, tools, skydiving, alcohol, driving motor vehicles, winding roads, and countless products, items, and services. These warnings, alerts and cautions exist to inform and safeguard consumers, users, businesses, and corporations from danger and lawsuits.

As warnings and training exist to protect life and property and minimize damage and loss associated with products and services, the same or greater care is called for in the arena of criticism to assure that personal experiences have minimal damage and harm and, instead, have mutually beneficial outcomes that enrich relationships.

The daily doses of dangers and harm done to relationships from criticism (as well as poor communication in general) somehow seem to be hidden by oblivion, conscious or willing blindness, and are less obvious than the dangers of explosives, plastic bags, jaywalking, chain saws, scuba diving or white-water rafting.

Is it because relationships are generally taken for granted by circumstances of birth, family life, socioeconomic-political factors, demographic realities, designations, or predetermined decisions? Is it because these and other factors outrank relationships and are consequently less valued than the dangers of explosives? Relationship damage can have long-lasting social, psychological, religious, political, financial, and physical effects for individuals, families, organizations, and nations, even for generations. Domestic violence, divorce, child abuse, gang activities (across the socioeconomic spectrum), bullying (by adults and children), some laws, polluted water, some zoning, war, and terror are all relationship issues and are often regarded as the way life is or something to get over, or they are dismissed as being as good as it gets—because it could be worse. If these factors cause economic decline to a certain level or point or another calamity occurs with economic impetus, then attention is given and some actions are taken for that situation.

We seem to be more expectant and hopeful of having positive outcomes from products that fail than we do of failed or disappointing relationships. It's as if we know the products will get better through upgrades and modifications, yet the social order seems doomed to failure or we tolerate less than what could be when it comes to relationships.

Valuing and enhancing relationships can decrease tension, lower stress, reduce the negative impact of criticism, and provide more space, energy, and time to build harmonious experiences and repair relationships. One way to value and enhance relationships is to analyze our thoughts, speech, and actions and responsibility toward ourselves and others with an awareness of how life can be better for all—given that we are inextricably connected and interdependent.

Please post the following universally relevant warnings relative to criticism in your mind and thoughts and be influenced by them as you contemplate presenting criticism or responding. Also, share this with others in the most appropriate manner.

> There is one whose rash words are like sword thrusts but the tongue of the wise brings healing.
> —Proverbs 12:18 KJV

> Harsh words stir up anger, a soft answer turns away wrath.
> —Proverbs 15:1 KJV

> Life and death are in the power of the tongue.
> —Proverbs 18:21 KJV

Count the cost! Improve relationships! Reduce conflict, bitterness, hatred and lawsuits! Make criticism a gift?

Warning summary

Communication (verbal and nonverbal), once transmitted, cannot be retrieved. Apologies and regrets will not, cannot, undo the impact of what was said or done nor what was not said or not done. I like to keep in mind the Miranda ruling in law which basically says, whatever you say (or not) can be used against you.

The information in this book will enhance our care, skill, and use of the tools and instruments of criticism (which is an element of communication), both as initiators (critics) and respondents (critizens). Implementation and application of the concepts and skills, along with responsibility, will prevent or minimize endless rounds of regret, countless bouts of turmoil and angst due to wrestling with "if only" and "I should have," or innumerable instances of being numb to the damage done from reckless criticism while searching for suitable scapegoats. Be proactive and count the cost of your words and actions or inactions in advance. Then act to achieve the best outcome for all parties by becoming skilled and proficient in the realm of criticism as a vital element of communication. Do this just as if you were handling nitroglycerin or a steak knife. Balancing and caring about what we say and the way we say it (the freedom of speech) with thought about the possible consequences (the power and responsibility) of such speech will move us toward harmony. This is communication 2.0.

Be an artist!

Be a relationship architect—use the tools of criticism to plan, design, build and maintain harmonious relationships.

The next chapter spells out the process and transition that helps bring about the change.

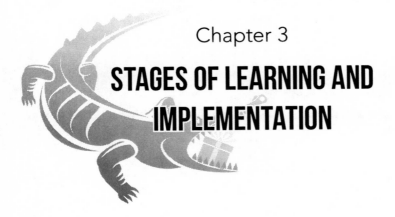

Chapter 3
STAGES OF LEARNING AND IMPLEMENTATION

The Path of Change

Whenever new or significantly different concepts, thoughts, and ideas are presented, varying degrees of resistance, acceptance, and opposition are to be expected. Change—while consistently constant—is often unpleasant, unappreciated, and sometimes painful. Change is a dynamic constant. These or similar feelings are expressed when I speak about criticism being more than an expression of disapproval and that it can be a gift benefitting all parties concerned.

Change often happens in four steps as part of the learning process in practically every realm of life and endeavor. These steps occur on the conscious and subconscious levels of mindedness—be it learning to walk, reading, riding a bicycle, learning a language or a new language, mastering new software, playing golf, or presenting and responding to criticism for mutually beneficial outcomes.

Brief exercise: Take a moment right now and fold your arms across your chest. It probably feels comfortable. Notice the hand (i.e., left) that is resting on top of your right upper arm and the other hand (i.e., right) resting under the left upper arm. Now reverse the fold. Your left hand is now under your right upper arm and the right hand is on top of the left upper arm. How does that feel? Most people express some degree of discomfort—even though it's their same arms and hands in a *different* position.

The change process sets the stage for expanded goals, dreams, and experiences or options. Dogged resistance and opposition to change provide assurance that the status quo will prevail.

Many people will opt to fold their arms in the way that feels comfortable. Status quo. Some will intentionally begin to fold their arms in the way that feels uncomfortable and experience this option (difference) until either way feels comfortable.

All new undertakings have a learning curve that happens through a sequence of repeated efforts, feedback, correction, and new attempts, each building upon the other, leading to achievement. Patience, intention, feedback, and persistence with self and others are active elements of the process, even when something goes awry.

The development of the theory and model of the four stages is dated from the 1970s and is associated with clinical psychologist Dr. Thomas Gordon founder of Gordon Training International and an employee by the name of Noel Burch. There is some discussion that Abraham Maslow of Brandeis University and Columbia University may have some association with the model.

The relevance and application of these stages are nearly universal and illustrated with the diagram used by Ralph G. Nichols, known as the "father of listening" and a major contributor to the development of the International Listening Association. A central theme of Dr. Nichols's is his belief that the greatest need of humans is to understand and to be understood, and that understanding occurs through listening.

A firm grasp of this model reminds us that learning is a process - in any area or discipline and involves a degree of tension and anxiety. It is a process, not an event. There are stages (a dynamic process) that need not be a state (static).

The diagram below reveals the associated levels of consciousness as the learner moves from merely being informed about a topic (new presentation and response to criticism) to the integrated level of unconscious competence.

Stages of Learning and Implementaion

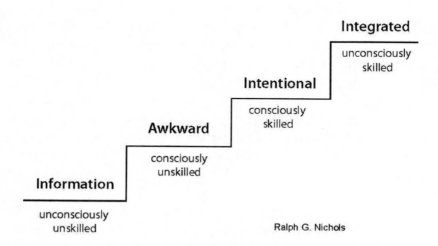

These stages occur with any new, different, or renewed experience. Incorporation and competency will follow the path of these four stages. The awkward stage is often the greatest challenge because it announces with clarity the discomfort, unfamiliarity, current weakness, or dislike of the call for change. (e.g., folding arms across your chest). Movement between each stage may require upward of twenty-one iterations.

Another example that illustrates the change process is a very familiar activity experienced by lots of people in many places globally. I refer to driving a motor vehicle by a first-time driver, one who has never operated a motor vehicle. The driver can be fifteen or fifty. Once all the permissions, approvals, and insurance requirements are met, the student enrolls in driver's education, attends all the classes, passes all the written exams with a score of 100. At this stage, the student only has information about driving. This is **stage 1** where the student does not know that he or she does not know how to drive.

Stage 2 is where the student gets behind the wheel to drive for the very first time with a parent, older sibling, friend, or a professional driving instructor. Without fail, emotions will vary from clumsy, awkward, embarrassing to nausea, anxiety, or panic. Many first-time drivers get nervous or shaky. Some become sick to the stomach. Some break out in sweat. Others' feet and hands may shake uncontrollably. This is the **awkward** stage. Some are so uncomfortable they become faint and must wait for a few minutes, an hour, or another day before they can resume with driving the vehicle—clumsily. This is for a vehicle that has an automatic transmission. If it has a stick or manual shift transmission, the challenge is magnified. The awkwardness is a significant and unavoidable part of learning to drive.

An instructor with skill and compassion understands what is happening and will support the student to ensure that he becomes a safe, competent, successful driver. The new driver eventually moves around the parking lot and later onto the roadway and "drives" awkwardly. The New Driver sign on the bumper or rear window alerts other drivers to be considerate. This clumsy, awkward feeling and experience is unavoidable if one is going to become a competent driver. Those who are too wary, fearful, and avoidant of the pain and discomfort of the awkward stage may seek to escape it—and may never drive.

Learning to face and embrace the temporary awkwardness empowers one to move from information to action. As time goes by, he or she gains more confidence, skills, and experience to drive intentionally and arrives at stage 3. Here he or she may be hesitant while thinking about what to do, with self-prompts: signal before changing lanes, drive in the right lane, pass in the left, the three-second count in following another vehicle, and so on. Driving a stick shift requires thinking and coordination for changing gears, stopping, and taking off. With continued practice, he or she learns to ease the clutch out when taking off on a hill without rolling back. Eventually he or she becomes more skilled and confident, learning to drive on a variety of roads, in different types of traffic and weather conditions, as well as different vehicles. Continually gaining skill and confidence moves the once-new driver through each phase sequentially to the integrated level or stage 4 on the consciousness scale. This is the stage of the expert who has learned and achieved and is now skilled and competent. This driver's thinking will be fluid and smooth. Each driver can achieve the integrated level at a pace that is right for him or her.

Note: Arriving at stage four can possibly lead to a state of complacency, when one becomes less attentive to the matter at hand and more easily distracted. I call this stage 5 where danger and disaster can occur. Learning and growth ceases where the person who once was eager to learn and sacrifice rests content as if there is nothing more to learn or is annoyed by the suggestion of continued growth and development. Not knowing that no one knows all there is to know about all there is to know. To avoid this stage after reaching a destination, rest for a while, enjoy, and celebrate. Then look around and wonder what lies beyond the horizon. Reach beyond your grasp!

Appeal: Stay alert with intentional reminders, purposeful attention, and action!

Learning to skillfully present and receive criticism involves the same four stages referenced earlier. This book is stage 1, which contains information about criticism, looking at our unique inherited attitude and use of and response to criticism as well as the developed intent and usage. Becoming familiar with the intent and process leads to implementation of the information progressing through stages two, three, and four. Please be assured that the discomfort or awkward feelings of the process is evidence that learning is happening, equipping and empowering us with warnings, potential benefits, and examples to make criticism a gift. With continued practice (stages two, three and four) comes improved understanding and movement toward mutually beneficial outcomes from criticism. This is the path to the paradigm shift that will improve your communication and consequently your relationships.

The next chapter is on the topic of communication and the requisite role it plays in making criticism a gift—criticism 2.0.

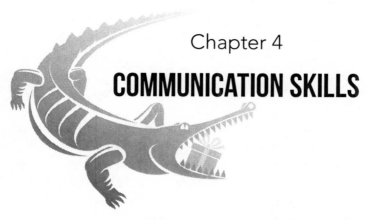

Chapter 4

COMMUNICATION SKILLS

The Lifeblood and Foundation of Relationships

The following chapters present skills and concepts to employ in planning, designing and building relationships—with intention, attention, responsibility, and accountability to oneself and those that comprise the relationship network. Stories are included to help illustrate the practical applications involved in presenting and responding to criticism for mutually beneficial outcomes. Relationships are established and improved when listening skills are above par with speaking, reading, and writing skills. The value and level of communication skills directly correlate to the value of relationships. Relationship value gaps tend to correlate with the level of communication skill and competence.

Keen listening, patience (*wait* training), and practice enhance insight and comprehension, resulting in better understanding of perceptions and experiences. This is critically important when presenting or responding to criticism, because it can lead to more harmony and improved relationships with our partners in life.

Many relationships may be taken for granted by the masses, and unconsciously regarded as a sort of a side effect of birth, and established by situations, geographical location, employment, school, economics, and so on.

Communication is to relationships as breathing is to being alive. Communication is so prevalent, common and important that it is often taken for granted in the context of relationships.

Taking the link between communication and relationship for granted can be likened to taking our physical health for granted. Wishing things would improve in the body, citing ads, commercials, products, services, and guarantees: while steadfastly avoiding or denying the necessary actions, changes and sacrifice necessary to achieve the stated desire.

It is actually change that brings about change.

The bodies we all live in function best when all the systems and networks communicate effectively. Optimal cell communication results in optimal operation of the body. When communication between cells is damaged, blocked, or compromised, there is a corresponding block or compromise in the functioning and operation of the body. When communication between and among people is skilled, appropriate, and respectful, there is a great possibility of relationship harmony and better functioning. When communication is poor, intermittent, or nonexistent the relationships that form or not are a direct correlation.

Bringing about changes in relationships dynamics is more likely to happen when there is a change in communication processes and practices. Hoping, wishing, and even praying for a change in marriage, family, employment, congregation, or social group while doggedly denying that a change in the manner of communication on your part might help is most likely to yield stagnation or decline of the relationship. Keep in mind that the change process is accompanied by awkward elements (as evidence of change in process) of discomfort and pain—be that physical, psychological, social, or mental/emotional.

A general lack of awareness and emphasis of this vital link is commonplace and causes many people to discredit and devalue training and instruction on this topic, thus contributing to a normalized complacency, as if we are doomed to muddled relationships because we are human. Few among the masses seem to be aware of the nature and power of communication and the overall impact on our relationships, professionally, socially, and otherwise. Family members, communities, congregations, schools, organizations, businesses, and governments seem to focus on relationships from a competition, testing, winning-and-losing angle. Assuring that there are winners and losers is more likely to yield inimical relationships rather than mutually beneficial ones. Many regard skills training in communication as a "necessary evil" imposed by management in businesses, a spouse in a domestic situation, or someone in a position of authority rather than an essential element of daily life and living and a primary element of relationship development. Training in communication can be perpetual and enriching throughout our lives.

Since no one knows all there is to know about all there is to know, there are boundless areas of exploration, discovery and learning that provide perpetual opportunities to grow beyond our grasp as we reach and extend beyond. Browning summarized in his saying:

> A man's reach should exceed his grasp.
> —Robert Browning

I see this saying applied as an extension ladder resting on the roofline of the house. In order for me to get up to the roof, I properly position the ladder, place my feet on the bottom rung, and grasp the appropriate rung with my hands. I climb higher by releasing one hand and reaching to the next rung up, going higher, putting my feet on the next rung, and climbing. This process of grasping, releasing, and reaching applies to multiple areas of life in numerous realms, including communication skills. Knowledge can be amended, modified, and improved upon in order to broaden life experiences. I want to learn perpetually by observing, testing, and analyzing, and from those who specialize in the world of communication with training programs and seminars for people in categories such as counseling, social work, psychology, customer service, and the like. Yet, the wide-ranging public lacks knowledge and skills in the basics of communication and relationship formation and development. Thus, by neglect or intention, many of the social ills experienced daily in practically all areas of endeavor multiply.

Here's what Shelle Rose Charvet, in her book *Words That Change Minds*, says,

> Poor communication is today's number one problem at work, at home and in the world at large. Discords among people are frequent, from small annoyances like twenty-minute phone mail messages, to lifelong parent-child resentments, to intractable conflicts between nations.

A therapist says,

> More that ninety percent of my clients suffering from depression, anxiety or other mental illness have one primary complaint—relationship problems at work or at home.

The point to be made here is that relationships are directly affected by the communication of the parties. Skill in presenting and responding to criticism can enhance relationships.

Recently, someone in a challenging situation (call him Frank) said to me, "I would give anything to make the situation better!" The conversation flowed as follows. Frank and I are indicated by F and B in the script.

> F—I would give anything to make this situation better.
>
> B—You would give anything to make it better. *(Restate and reflect)*
>
> F (pauses before continuing)—Well, it be worth a lot for that to happen.
>
> B—What would it be worth to you? *(It is important to wait for the response)*
>
> F (spousal relationship)—If we could just talk without resorting to scoring points on who's right or wrong, and without always referring to things that have happened in the past, and one of us feeling defeated, then the winner of the argument begins to feel bad for defeating the other. Afterward, there is a period of withdrawal (lasting a couple of days or a week). Then some occasion like a party, dinner, or other public event comes along, giving us the impetus to come out of withdrawal to get ready for the event—as if nothing happened that brought on the withdrawal. No discussion, reference, acknowledgment, or change, we have a great time—until the next time. These things build and multiply and become more intense with each episode.
>
> It would be worth our family and peace of mind.
>
> (church meeting)—If we could manage to have a meeting and stay on topic as spelled out in the agenda, without bringing up matters that have been repeatedly discussed ad nauseam without resolution, and adjourn at a decent hour feeling like we'd made progress. It feels like a monthly spinning

wheel. The change would be relief from distress and anticipatory anxiety for the two weeks prior and the week following the meeting.

B—You say you would give anything for this to happen, is that correct?

F (pause)—Yes!

B—Are you willing to do what it takes to begin the process?

At this point, the pace of the conversation slowed, and Frank's breathing rate changed, and his posture relaxed. Now the invitation could be presented for him to be the agent who promoted the changes he said he wanted. It would begin with a change in manner and presentation of his communication. If he committed to being the change agent, the next step was to present instruction and commence training in communication concepts, skills, and practices. This is the foundation comprised of the right elements/components for the unique situation, patience, and time.

Just as the foundation of a house, building, or bridge is critical and essential—comprised of specific materials, expertise, skill, inspection, and time to assure the integrity, safety, service, comfort and maintenance of the structure, and understanding that everything in the building or on the bridge rests on the foundation, likewise, a stable foundation and maintenance are essential in determining the health and stability of relationships. Communication is the foundation – firm and solid, yet flexible, adaptable and essential. These are not *soft skills*. It requires specific skills, training, and assistance from others who can help test and inspect the elements of a person's style, approach, and skill level (infrastructure). A certain amount of time is required for changes to form and set in place, depending upon the individual's willingness and ability to change, learn, and grow beyond where they are. The outcome is likely to be a better, stronger, more stable, and more flexible foundation/relationship.

Here are some examples of communication and its corresponding impact on a relationship.

Let's say Ted has an emotional reaction to wasting water. While in a public bathroom, he sees someone in the process of washing his hands in the prescribed manner. The person turns the water on, lathers his hands with soap, scrubs for twenty seconds, and rinses. Then the person turns and starts talking to someone while the water is still running.

Before going into the lecture mode, Ted is opting to breathe and assess the situation, including the running water. Before acting, ask internally, "Is it worth giving them a lesson or lecture—especially when others are present—about the value of this precious element, insisting or demanding that they refrain from such wastefulness?" **Consider the relationship**, whether stranger or friend. Though nearly frustrated by seeing and hearing the water running down the drain, ponder: is there likely another time, place, or approach that can be more mutually beneficial? Assess the critizone (the situation, setting, and the relationship) and choose to act based on the best chances for a mutually beneficial outcome. Bear in mind that the means and method of the communication will set the frame and parameters of the relationship. Maybe in this instance, the amount of wasted water will likely not warrant damaging or perhaps ruining the relationship or setting in concrete a negative impact. There may be another place and time that could be better to talk about this rather than going with the impulse in that moment. Consider the proverb that says,

> The first to present his case seems right, till another comes forward and questions him.
>
> —Proverbs 18:17 RSV

Situations sometimes occur where the benefits of *not speaking* prove to be of greater value than merely citing the facts to prove who is right or wrong. Here are a few instances where I spoke and received confirmation afterward that it would have been better had I waited to speak, or maybe not spoken at all.

Situation 1

I was installing a towel rack in the bathroom. My wife, Edwina, wanted it in a location between the window and the shower. (I did not confirm the spot with her I merely logged it in my mind and continued).

> Bill: Okay, got it. (Merrily, I install the screw and place the rack on it.)
>
> Edwina (points to a different location with her index finger): This is where I want it—not there.
>
> Bill (feeling irritated at the gesture and tone in which she spoke, responds impulsively): If I am not putting it where you want, perhaps you can put it up.

Well, as you might be imagining, there ensued a bit of banter that lasted at least seven or eight minutes about who meant what, compounded by more verbal and nonverbal communication. Two other proverbs are instructive.

> When words are many, transgression is not lacking, but he who restrains his tongue is prudent.
>
> —Proverbs 10:19 KJV

> The more words, the more vanity, and how does that benefit anyone?
>
> —Ecclesiastes 6:11 (modified)

The time spent arguing and attempting to prove who was right or wrong (this is an example of the win/lose circular-pattern phenomenon) took more time than it would have taken to hang the rack. Additionally, it took another hour or so to address the wounds. Had I counted the cost and asked the question internally, "Is this the hill I want to die on?" I would have merely marked the spot I thought she'd meant and, when she'd indicated a change, made the change, mounted the rack, and moved on to the next project.

A few changes I could have made are listed below:

1) When she first indicated where she wanted the rack, I could have
   - confirmed the location and marked the spot before putting in the anchor and screw (restate and reflect); or
   - asked her to mark the spot.
2) When she pointed, and stated the preferred location, I could have
   - acknowledged and confirmed the new location, or
   - made the correction without commentary or grumbling.

Situation 2

Then there was the time when someone (let's call her Edriene) criticized me during a meeting with fifteen people present. She had been very critical of me for about a year regarding a decision I had made about staff positions. I was satisfied with the decision and felt it was objective and right for the circumstances. Edriene did not get the position she desired. Since that time, she had spoken subtleties about me and other decisions I was making, using innuendo and indirect references as to my motives.

The meeting referenced above took place nearly a year after the staffing decision was made. At some point during the meeting, as my youngest daughter was speaking, Edriene cut her off in mid statement, said she was merely a child, and then directed her speech to me as follows:

> Edriene (in loud voice with rigid body language): You and your elders don't care anything about this congregation. It's all a power play to keep certain people in and others out.

I instantly felt a very rare surge of anger and reacted loudly in front of all those gathered, two of whom were my children. I was so angry that I was momentarily afraid of myself. In that moment, I stood up as a way of managing my emotions through a physical action, and I spoke with loud intensity. Apparently, at that point my youngest daughter left the meeting.

> Bill: I am only going to make this statement once. Stop badgering me! I recognize that you are other than pleased with me being the pastor and that you differ with my plans and style of leadership. I say this based on our previous conversations about the elders and other matters. To raise this issue in this meeting is totally inappropriate and unacceptable.

Sandi, a member and officer who had taken some communication skills training from me, spoke up.

> Sandi: It seems that we have gotten off track from the purpose and agenda for this meeting. I would like to suggest that the two of you complete your conversation at another time and place.
> (brief pause)
> Let's decide as a group to either go back to the agenda or adjourn this meeting and set a follow-up date to complete our committee work.

Sandi's intervention provided time for me to defuse and regain control of myself and my composure and to participate with the group as they decided to complete the agenda.

After the meeting was adjourned, I went directly to Edriene and asked her to talk to me—which she did. Following this conversation, I didn't see my younger daughter. No one knew where she was. Her sister said she had left the meeting soon after Edriene had made her remarks.

I went on a search and found her in my office, sobbing. She expressed that she felt embarrassed and humiliated about what was said to her and that it was said in front of everyone. At the conclusion of her statement I spoke to her.

> Bill: Let's go back to the room so you can tell Edriene how you feel before she leaves.
>
> Daughter: Dad it's okay, I'll get over it. Maybe I should have kept silent and not said anything.
>
> Bill: You are a member of the committee and entitled to speak. I want you to face her now so there is nothing to get over. Come with me now.
>
> Daughter: I really don't want to. I already feel bad.
>
> Bill: I will be with you while you tell her. Once you do this, you will feel better.
>
> Daughter: Oh, all right.

The two of them talked. Edriene apologized for disrespecting her and acknowledged that she was a full member of the committee. My daughter felt better. For the remainder of my stay as the pastor, there were no more confrontations with Edriene and me.

In situation 2, Sandi's application of the appropriate skills addressed the emotional and factual elements and helped defuse the situation. I calmed down to a point where I could express myself in a professional and proper way. I then addressed the facts and my feelings to all present. The damage to the relationships of those present and others with whom it was shared took energy and time to repair. There wasn't much restoration with me and Edriene. There was a sort of mutual toleration. The shelf life lingers, and the lessons learned then prove beneficial to me today.

At some point in time following this event, I came upon a book that helped me better prepare for situations that might otherwise prompt a spontaneous or impulsive response or reaction by considering six options for the situation at hand. The book is by Terry Dobson and Victor Miller and is titled *Aikido in Everyday Life*. They apply the philosophy and techniques of martial arts in a physical threat—to communication and relationships. The basic options to a threat are:

1. Fight back (usually the last option)
2. Withdrawal
3. Parley
4. Do nothing
5. Deception (distraction if you prefer)
6. Aiki (confluence)

Begin with the option that is the most considerate of the other and the least costly to repair if there is damage.

Example

While visiting friends in the Philadelphia area, a discussion arose regarding the depth of the swimming pool at the deep end. I had been in the pool and had gone to the bottom. As the discussion ensued, I felt certain that the depth was eight feet—based on my experience. A couple of people who had been in this pool many times over the years said it was ten feet. My immediate internal thought was, "That's not right." Next, using my *wait* training skills, I considered the situation (critizone) and came up with the following options, keeping in mind that this was a matter of relative insignificance—and needed not be a cause of distress:

1) Debate the depth of the pool based on my experience with the emphasis that I am right (fight back).
2) Listen to the discussion of those who are more knowledgeable of the pool than am I (withdrawal or do nothing).
3) Go in the pool and show them (parley or fight back based on how I go about this).

4) Suggest that someone go measure the depth (parley).
5) Ignore this aspect of the discussion and enjoy the time with the people (distraction).
6) Say nothing and wait to see what happens (do nothing).

As this matter persisted throughout the day, with specific guests engaged in playful banter, the host got the skimming pole and asked someone who was in the pool to put it on the bottom and mark the depth. That settled the matter and everyone accepted the measurement (confluence). There was nothing to apologize for and no need for me to say anything at all about the depth of the pool.

In some instances, waiting and observing can yield valuable information that is given freely without probing. This calls for *wait* training: checked ego, assessment and context, patience, keen and attentive observation.

In the case of an urgent critical situation, *wait* training is disregarded in the interest of safety and preservation of life. If someone is struggling to stay afloat in the pool, immediate lifesaving action is required. This would be an exception to waiting and seeking the multiple options that might or might not be available.

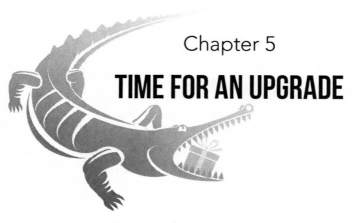

Chapter 5

TIME FOR AN UPGRADE

For communication and relationships!

An upgrade regarding criticism skills requires a modification in mind-set, attitude, and practices. This book and the references cited herein provide options for presenting and responding to criticism. New or different thoughts and attitudes about yourself and others will develop and lead to new practices. To install this upgrade requires that your computer (mind, body, brain, and spirit) be restarted (reevaluate your view toward criticism). Question your resistance to changing, learning, and growing beyond previously set and accepted boundaries. You have the option of doing that now or waiting until the next power outage (relationship meltdown) or another forced restart. It's about attitude, belief, practices, and a willingness to reconsider the benefits of an age-old issue.

See Proverbs 23:7, KJV version:

As we think in our hearts so we become.

The following statement on the marquee at the Holocaust Museum in Washington, DC, is worthy of contemplation: Think about what you say!

There are many ways to improve communication skills. Attending workshops seminars, and classes, going to conferences, reading books, magazines, articles, and other publications, and watching videos as well as online trainings is encouraged. Additionally, one can begin improving their communication skills on their own by taking a few minutes a day to practice presenting and responding to criticism and other communication skills and techniques using a mirror. This exercise is best done when you are alone.

Mirror exercises

Go to a mirror, stand or sit and look at yourself. If you find this awkward or uncomfortable, it's primarily because it's new and different. (A review of the previous chapter can be helpful with new learning experiences.) Focusing on your own eyes in the mirror is a deep, powerful experience that many people find extremely challenging. Yet it can be a significant reach to an inner depth of connection with self.

Suggested initial exercise. Think of an experience with a friend, family member, or coworker that was pleasant and enjoyable. Breathe and relax your shoulders. (Refer to page 55 for information on diaphragmatic breathing.) Spend some time observing and noting responses in your body from this pleasant experience. Notice your skin tone, eyes, neck, breathing pattern, feelings in your gut, and other bodily expressions. It is helpful to learn and know the meaning of your body's biochemical and electromagnetic signals. Do this often enough to get a sense of what it is like and what you can learn about yourself before moving to a more challenging mirror exercise with criticism.

More challenging exercise. Before doing this exercise complete several iterations of the exercise above. This will give you a feel for the mirror and you. Now think of a sensitive or delicate observation, opinion or criticism you would like to present to a particular person or group, or a response to a criticism that was presented to you. Be clear and specific about the individual, the topic and the criticism. Take some time and write out the criticism. Rewrite it at least three times making alterations and changes with each rewrite to improve the criticism or the response.

Alert: Please reread and rewrite your texts and e-mails
before sending. It could be a great benefit.

At the mirror—when and where it is feasible—speak your words and thoughts aloud as you practice your presentation. Look at yourself in the mirror. Get in touch with yourself by gazing into your eyes. Breathe and calm yourself. Relax your shoulders.

What does the mirror tell you about you? Continue practicing, going through the four stages of learning until you feel comfortable with that which is new and different. The four stages were presented in the previous chapter. If you want to, place a bookmark here, review and refresh the information on the four stages of learning, and then return to this page.

Use the mirror in the same manner as above to respond to a criticism that someone has shared with you. Write out your response; visualize the person and your response to him/her. What does your response say to you about you? Continue practicing until you feel comfortable making your response.

If there is no pending real-life situation, do an imaginary scenario. The practice will be helpful for facing a real-life situation at some point in the future. This process can also be helpful in resolving any number of unsettled or annoying past issues. Practice regularly even if no criticism or response is on the horizon. It will come. Practice will allow you to improve how you present and respond to criticism in advance of a real-life situation

As you practice, the intensity of the awkward feelings will begin to subside as your presentation and response skills are enhanced.

I hope you find this exercise helpful. There are additional uses of the mirror to address self-esteem and identity which are quite beneficial and can be addressed in another forum. And as stated earlier in this chapter, please seek classes, training programs and other means of learning about communication skills. These learnings can lead to intentional communication with a goal of harmony among parties, versus impulsive competition.

The call for intentional communication with associated warnings goes out to parents, educators, grandparents, daycare providers, healthcare professionals, and others who work with and are around children as well as any person. Value relationships even in critical or challenging situations because this can be an opening for a paradigm shift for all those involved in the matter. Do a personal assessment of your communication style, your history of encounters and experiences that involved criticism as critic and critizen. This can be regarded as reviewing our communication/criticism album—akin to looking at a photo album. Such reviews can reveal things that have always been present—though not seen previously.

- What is the pattern and nature of such experiences?
- What are your default responses when the critic is a family member, coworker, boss or supervisor, close friend, teacher, coach, mentor, or stranger? Has it occurred to you that you have different

default positions or responses, depending on various elements of the critizone?

- What does this say about your value of relationships?
- What is the integrity of the foundation (communication)?
- What are the infrastructure or maintenance factors?
- Do you have a therapist?

Awareness of these elements provides beneficial feedback, leading to change, that dynamic constant.

Yes, people can change—some will change the world!

Change often occurs through awareness of a need, a demand to change or an interest in changing through various impetuses.

Be Alert to Patterns of Behavior

A useful resource to help bring awareness of patterns in behavior and relationships that could benefit from change is the scale of prejudice and discrimination developed in 1954 by the late Dr. Gordon Allport of Harvard University. His work is relevant to criticism, because in many instances, whether intended or not, the effects of bias, prejudice, and discrimination, expressed in harsh judgment or by those in positions of authority, are frequently experienced by the citizen. It is possible that some presentations and responses to criticism are a result of inherited cultural and social norms based on bias and prejudice.

Allport's five-point scale begins with something that is very common, popular, and all-too-often socially acceptable with no apparent awareness of the deep impact, warnings, or likely enduring shelf life, and little or no responsibility. That is name-calling, which includes teasing, joking and kidding around. I have amended Dr. Allport's list to include gossip, bullying, and hazing. Bullying and hazing and are cited by PubMed.gov as lethal *maltreatment.*

- Antilocution: Name-calling, teasing, joking, put-downs, humiliation *(added by this author are: bullying, humor intended to hurt, and careless or reckless criticism)*
- Avoidance or isolation
- Discrimination

- Violence against people, animals, or property
- Extermination

When it comes to criticism, I want to post warning messages and thoughts on mirrors, desks, walls in schools and office buildings, on bulletin boards, on automobile dashboards, athletic centers, streaming messages on TV, and other places, warnings akin to those used in handling nitro and other products. Be mindful that intent, design, context, amount, and placement are significant factors that determine success or disaster. Please bear in mind that what may be innocent "fun" to some can be taken as a value judgment by another. Some have committed suicide from teasing and bullying.

Critics can be callous and heartless—crushing the spirit of the critizen, sometimes unaware of the hurt and pain they cause, and sometimes criticizing with intention to hurt another. Critics equipped with skills, tact, options, and a heart for people can be effective in presenting an opinion or criticism that respects the other person and yield mutually beneficial outcomes.

Critizens can likewise be callous and heartless in their own defense and respond in kind to the critic, stoking the fires of bitterness or hostility. Critizens equipped with skill, tact, options, and a heart for people can respond to criticism in ways that move toward mutually beneficial outcomes.

Either or both can be resolute in speaking their minds (freedom of speech) with no sense of responsibility for what or how they speak, fueled only by their determinations to win by fighting verbally or physically. Likewise, either or both can speak and act with a sense of duty to stretch themselves beyond their comfort zones and move to a place of harmony and be responsible for their speech in consideration of themselves and others.

Here are examples of harmful use of an observation, opinion or emotional outburst that can be interpreted/experienced as criticism. I stress that these are things that have happened, and I encourage you to avoid them. Many of you may have been spoken to or perhaps you have spoken in this way.

- What is wrong with you?
- I don't know what is wrong with you!

- Can't you do anything right?
- You should be ashamed of yourself!
- Oh, just forget it!
- I am sick and tired of you!
- A mother said to her teenage daughter during a heated argument, "I should have aborted you!"
- A mother said to her daughter, one of nine children, "I'd rather have eight more boys than another girl like you."
- Who made you the judge about anything?

There are people who say things like this while physically hitting, pushing, shoving, or beating the critizen, making it seem that the criticism and the punishment are connected or at least linked together.

Critizens have displayed shock, some experience breathlessness, and still others have felt despair and hopelessness when confronted by a critic as a domineering figure (parent, teacher, spouse, significant other, boss, church officer, politician, public official, etc.) who expresses him- or herself with statements akin to those above. Some critizens retaliate with defensive responses and initiate or maintain the cycle of hostility.

Criticism can be carefully crafted and presented with the intent to bring aid to the critizen seeking a mutually beneficial outcome. The warnings in this book call attention to the potential dangers of impulsive presentations and responses with no sense of responsibility and offer insight and direction to empower or aid both/all parties.

Examples

Here are some examples of interactions between critic and critizen. Read them aloud or ask someone to role-play them with you. After completing these examples, please share and discuss the outcomes. Then apply the suggestions and concepts of mutually beneficial outcomes to situations in your life. Keep in mind that there are harsh and soft words. Words that hurt or words that heal. Consider which is likely to move toward harmony and mutuality? There are consequences for each approach.

Critic
- I expected that the trash would be emptied by the time I came home.

Or

- You didn't take the trash out!

Critic
- Can I offer you a mint?

Or
- Your breath stinks!

The critizen likewise can either fan or squelch the flames of criticism. Here are a few examples:

- You want to know what is wrong with me—it's you!

Or
- It seems that I have disappointed you in some way.
- No matter what I do it's never right in your sight anyway.

Or
- My grades are less than you expected and I may not get the scholarship. This must be disappointing.
- Well since you didn't abort me and you wish you had, I guess it would be all right for me to kill myself.

Or
- This argument has taken us to a different place. Do you really feel that way?

Movement toward a mutually beneficial outcome in the realm of criticism requires a level of skill and temperance that is representative of handling nitroglycerin. Both the critic and the critizen would do well to consider the elements of the critizone before presenting or responding to a criticism. Doing so can minimize disruption and maximize the possibility for understanding that may lead toward harmony.

Parents, spouses, significant others, grandparents, siblings, teachers, childcare providers, bosses, coworkers, coaches, and others can unintentionally convey a devaluing message with no idea or *intent* of doing so. Then defend their actions when informed of the *effect*. These same individuals can learn and apply basic and foundational communication skills with movement toward cooperation and harmony, thus minimizing or avoiding damage or other unintended consequences.

Regularly and routinely, the roles of critic and critizen alternate in a series of cycles toward a breakdown or stalemate, or toward resolution and harmony. Either party, the critic or critizen can determine the direction and impact. Bear in mind that criticism and a response (all communication) is nonverbal as well as verbal.

Gestures as well as statements made on a daily basis can affect the experiences of a child, teen, young adult, adult, spouse, business partner, choir members, or groups of people who may sense a devaluation or disapproval from a parent, sibling, or other relative, teacher, boss, preacher, or others. Some will more readily acknowledge the hurt verbally or nonverbally, while others will deny the hurt and respond by hunkering down in a retaliatory strike mind-set against the other person or group. The manner, tone, and nature of a verbal or nonverbal expression can have lasting effects on one's psyche, especially when the person believes the expression to be dismissive, signaling disappointment or incompetence.

One day in my office, John said to me, "Everything changed on that day. My parents treated me with a sense of distance, as did my siblings, and even the dog didn't like me anymore." He explained that this had been the day the teacher in elementary school called on him to respond to a question. When the student hesitated, the teacher quickly said, "Oh never mind", flipped her hand downward and to the side, rolled her eyes, turned her head and called on another student. His interpretation of this experience held a grip on John for nearly half a century. Fortunately, he got help, healing and release from captivity to his interpretation of the teacher's action.

A ninety-nine-year-old lady reported how statements made to her when she was a small child being cared for by a custodial aunt affected her sense of self all her life. The repetitive statements were "You're no good. You can't do anything right. You are always in the way." She reviewed her life accomplishments and recounted how her work had been lauded and praised by many in professional as well as nonprofessional arenas resulting in very good sales of her work, and the gifts she had bestowed upon those who were moved with gratitude—by the work she did. There were other achievements she recalled with pleasure and delight, yet the statements made by that aunt in her childhood had a haunting effect and stifling grip on her sense of self along the course of her journey. She made many attempts to "forget it," yet the thoughts lingered. To forget is almost impossible—especially absent some brain decline or trauma.

With some guidance, she decided to change the way she looked at her past with the aunt by looking at life from the aunt's perspective as best she could. The counselor facilitated a review of the aunt's past before she was placed in her aunt's care, some of the issues that influenced the aunt's life, and with some context, she reframed the experience and the meaning of the experience changed. She also agreed to remove a framed picture of her aunt from a wall shelf and placed it in a box. These actions empowered her to regain significant emotional confidence to break the imposed life commandment that had held her in a state of emotional and psychological incompetence as she approached the century age mark.

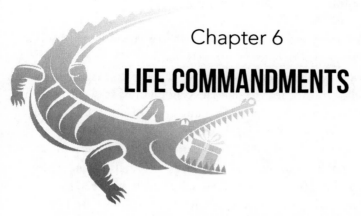

Chapter 6

LIFE COMMANDMENTS

This is a term I learned from Dr. Savage, defined as "the scripts we learn very early in life from family, community, religion, education, social, and other aspects of life that become the norm of how life is to be." They are often "foundational" due to the nature, manner of how they are conveyed, and repetitive experiences that support the teachings. There are positive and negative commandments.

A few examples of positive life commandments are

- I believe in you
- Well done!
- I love you!
- You can do it! I know you can!

Here are a few examples of negative life commandments:

- You will never amount to much
- I'd rather have eight more boys than a girl like you
- You're just like _____.
- Boys don't cry.
- Views toward certain people (name, skin color, religion, country of origin, etc.)
- You'll always be heavy—it runs in your family

Here's a couple of conceptual life commandments:

- When traveling by auto, we only stop when we need to buy gasoline. So use the restroom before we get started.
- The proper way to open a box of dry cereal is to peel the tabs of the label open (not tear it); cut the cellophane package; pour the cereal into a bowl; fold the cellophane and crease it; then tuck the tabs of the top into place.
- The proper way to clean the kitchen after a meal is to clear all items from the table, counter, and stove top. Wipe all surfaces clean. Wash and dry all dishes, pots, pans, and cutlery, sweep floor and mop if needed, and put away all dishes, pots, pans, and cutlery. Now the kitchen is clean for the next meal.

The following story reveals the depth of life commandments with little or no awareness of the relational impact on the formation or dissolution.

Marc and Anna

Anna was leaving an event in Chattanooga, driving her car to another function about twenty minutes away. She knew Marc was without transportation and graciously asked if he would like a ride since she was going near the place he had referenced earlier. He willingly agreed and expressed gratitude for the offer. Neither party mentioned time factors or routes to take (elements of the critizone).

Anna is aware of Marc's personality and tendency to display a know-it-all attitude about most things. (He has displayed this attitude and behavior seeming always and was rewarded by family and friends for his domineering ways.) However, she pushes that aside and makes the offer in a spirit of kindness and generosity. (She had been taught and encouraged to be considerate of others who might have a need that she can meet, even if it involved being temporarily inconvenienced or uncomfortable—life commandment.)

As Anna drove along engaged in conversation with her passenger, Marc abruptly interrupted and said, "Why didn't you take that road?" pointing to a road they'd just passed. She was confused and said, "This is the way I go when I drive to the park. You did say the place you wanted to go is near the park, right?"

The conversation continued as follows:

> Marc: Yes, I did say I wanted to go to the park, and I appreciate the ride. It's just that it would be a lot faster if you had turned back there.
> Anna: I didn't know there was a concern about time.
> Marc: Well, there really isn't. It's just that it will get us there quicker and save some gas if you turn around and go that way.
> Anna: What are you saying?
> Marc: What do you mean, what am I saying? I told you what I am saying. (Now speaking louder and in a staccato manner—fight-back option) We would get there quicker taking the other route. I thought you knew your way around town.
> Anna: Well, I'm sorry I offered you a ride. I'll remember to never do that again! Something like this always happens with you and believe me: this is the last time it will happen to me. I've had enough (withdrawal)(breaking of a life commandment).

Neither person spoke another word for the remainder of the trip, a trip that started out on a note of gratitude and was positive that turned harsh in an instant. Anna was regretting she'd ever made the offer, thinking, "There he goes again—he always has to be right even when he acknowledges that it doesn't matter." Marc was nearly seething at her refusal to take the route that he would have taken had he been driving, had he had a car. He is certain that route would take less time and save gas. He knows he's right, even when he acknowledges that it's a minor matter. Being right overrides the benefit of the ride.

Marc inherited a life commandment of debate and argue; compete and win; from his family and specific elements of his community, basically as a way of life. Facts and effects didn't figure much in that environment. Being right was the goal—no matter the cost or magnitude. Be it small or otherwise. There was competition just to get to talk and dominate the conversation or time of others. Winning the debate or argument was the chief objective. Relationships between and among friends and family were as they were because that's the way things were.

A rework of this experience follows, using the guidelines presented in part I of the chapter on assessment. Feel free to turn there now or after reading the rework of the experience. I'll replay the scene using the elements of the critizone and the skills called for by the situation. We will pick up at the point where Marc questions her route of travel.

> Marc (pointing to a road they've just passed): Why didn't you take that road?
>
> Anna (confused, begins to think about previous encounters with Marc. *There he goes again, always has to be right. Why did I ever offer him a ride? I don't have to be nice to him.* Reflecting on life commandment. Catches herself, takes a few diaphragmatic breaths): Please share the reason you are suggesting that I turn around and take another route?
>
> Marc: Well, it is quicker and shorter and will reduce the time to get there and save gas money.
>
> Anna: How much time will it save to turn around and go the other way?
>
> Marc: Well, maybe five minutes or so.
>
> Anna: Are you pressed to get there by a specific time?
>
> Marc: No, not really, I just like going that way.
>
> Anna (aware of her breath): Since we are on this route and there is no rush to get there, I will proceed on this route. Do you have any objection to my plan?
>
> Marc: Well, not really. I guess I'm just used to going the other way.
>
> Anna: Without further ado, let's enjoy the ride.

They ride along, with a subdued tone, casually commenting on the scenery and casual talk and arrived safely at the destination. There was no banter.

Let's consider another option based on Marc's continued insistence of Anna turning around and taking his preferred route.

> Anna (upon hearing several iterations of Marc's insistence that she turn around and take the other route, breathes and quickly considers her options): Marc, I am going to pull into the shopping center up ahead. I would like to clear this matter up because it is distracting from my attention to driving. (Parley)
>
> Marc: (silence prevails on his part)

Anna (when the car is parked in a safe area): I offered you a ride based on hearing your earlier conversation. I am glad to follow through on providing the ride. However, if you continue to insist that I turn around and take a different route merely because you want me to do so, I invite you to leave my car and call Uber, Lyft, or a cab. Please decide what you want to do?

This could be the end of the banter in this scenario.

However, if there is a more significant trip that involves a greater distance and a couple of hours of travel time and Marc suggesting an alternative route than Anna is driving, it might be beneficial to follow the suggestion below. In this scenario, Anna is going from Chattanooga, Tennessee, to Birmingham, Alabama. Marc sees that Anna is driving east on I-24 heading away from I-59.

Marc asks (rather than demands) about the intended route of travel and Anna continues on the route she is driving.

Marc (takes a few deep breaths, devoid of any audible sighs): May I ask about the planned route and ETA for arriving in Birmingham? (Parley)

Anna: Actually, I hadn't thought about those particulars. I am only familiar with this route. Do you have a recommendation or suggestion for an alternative route?

Marc: My rough calculations are that we can reduce our travel time by forty-five minutes by taking I-59 based on where we are right now by likely avoiding a lot of the slower traffic on I-24.

Anna: Okay. Are you willing to be the navigator?

Marc: Glad to do so.

More on Allport's Findings

Name-calling, teasing, labeling and reckless criticism can result in an individual or a group being isolated, then discriminated against. When these prevail, physical attack and other forms of violence can follow, with the potential outcome of extermination (physical, social, psychological, financial, etc.) This is not a mutually beneficial outcome.

Violent Language

The language used in sports by some coaches, players, supporters, sponsors, sportscasters, and fans, young and old, is replete with violent overtones and expressions, reinforced by their body language, with the apparent intent to diminish or devalue the other team, even in church leagues, school, city, or nation. Perhaps this is an influence toward destructive behavior (not just to defeat an opponent) but to triumph and defeat the designated enemy, for some athletes, fans, and supporters. Winning isn't enough. Sometimes the winner destroys something of the opponent's or their own property or town.

This language has mutated into many everyday conversations and discussion by many adults and adopted by children, breeding systemic practices, methods, and embedded life commandments that enable some to be free from responsibility when there is slander, lying, and harm.

Just because others laugh doesn't mean it's funny. Ridicule and its cousins are generally counterproductive to the personhood of self and others. In some cases, personal dignity can be destroyed; people die or can lose the awareness of the value of their own lives as well as the lives of loved ones, colleagues, and friends due to someone's sense of liberty or freedom to say whatever they want with no sense of responsibility for the consequences. Sometimes it is a matter of life and death.

In some organizations, businesses, some religious groups, clubs, gangs, sports and athletic teams there is a culture (life commandment) of shame and put down with the goal of absolute compliance by all employees and absolute defeat and triumph of competitors—as though there were enemies.

Many in the general public, children, teens, and adults, have incorporated violent terms, attitudes and actions, and apply them to whomever they choose, whenever they want, with very little or no consideration of the possible damaging consequences: sissy, dummy, show-off, what's wrong with you, lazy, bubble head, dumbbell, motor mouth, and other harsh words; slurs, vulgarity, demeaning ethnic, social and derisive sexual terms. Cruel depictions in cartoons, drawings, videos and songs add to the contagion of degrading language used toward other members of the human family.

Such attitudes and behavior demean, devalue, and dehumanize people, making it easier to move from name-calling to isolation to discrimination and sometimes to violence. Numerous tragedies have been perpetrated by someone "going postal" in venues beyond the post office.

The language of politics uses similar words and phrases. Some are warlike expressions, which can set up inimical views and perspectives of others versus a mere competitive attitude. Often there are warlike programs set up and promoted as being helpful to some people in some places. A war against poverty may turn out to be a war against impoverished people. A war against crime may prompt warlike attacks against people who commit crimes, or may be accused of committing crimes. And there's the war(s) against drugs—which is a war against some people who use, sell, or distribute drugs. And the drug epidemic grows, assuring that the war will be perpetuated. The books, articles, blogs, and debates about violent language and the First Amendment occupy a lot of space in the media. Below is the title of an article that conveys the point.

Fighting words: Violent political rhetoric fuels violent attitudes

By Jared Wadley

News Service Week of January 31, 2011

The Commercial Appeal—Memphis, Tennessee

Guest column: The dangers of violent political language

The danger of outrageous rhetoric is that it prepares a social context in which the unthinkable becomes possible.

Even in the realm of social media, phrases such as "shoot me an email," "hit me up," and other related terms affect our sub consciousness, lowering the threshold of awareness and impact, thus promoting the likelihood that violent attitudes, words, and actions are easier to express. So many people use the term "hanging" in there without any apparent reference to the violent and malevolent traditions and acts of hanging people as a social or in some instances a form of entertainment.

Chapter 7

FREEDOM OF SPEECH

Responsibility and Accountability

Writing this book is part of my contribution to teach and display responsibility of speech as a duty and condition of the right of speech. Freedom of speech does not provide freedom from hurt and damage from what is spoken to others or self. There are times when a word or phrase misspoken or spoken with little or no thought can spark a hostile or violent reaction. Freedom to speak is regarded as natural, even a law in some settings. Accountability and responsibility are like guardrails, limits or boundaries that protect the speaker and the listener, the critic and the critizen. When damage is done due to vile reckless speech, it is fitting that there be accountability often involving restitution or compensation for damage done to others from such speech. Some people will likely be exempt from penalties or avoid, evade, deter, maneuver around, or wait out lawsuits and countersuits because they have the resources.

The following exercise can be helpful for anyone who wishes to get in touch with the power of their speech, minimize the negatives, and accentuate the positives of their communication.

Make a list of potentially explosive and healing words that can tear a person down or build a person up. Which words have what impact on you? Are you aware of which words you are most likely to use?

Being aware of our thoughts and speech can lead to the development of new practices and direct us to comport ourselves in ways that exemplify the higher calling to be more fully human and alter embedded presuppositions and life commandments about people, behavior and nature, recognize and regard others as members of the universal—global human family. Our partners on the journey of life.

Parallels to Driving

The Critical Motorist

There are elements of driving that have some application to criticism 1.0—expressing disapproval, mistakes, or faults when drivers warn others or are themselves warned by the sound of a horn, screeching brakes or vocal expressions and are spared a crash. The result is positive for both parties—even though some may bristle at the warning.

Driving a motor vehicle is a risky venture, safely undertaken by tens of millions of people on a daily basis in this country and hundreds of millions around the globe. Drivers on the whole are better trained and tested to perform safely as operators of vehicles than as people with the freedom of speech to present or respond to criticism. Among the reasons for this are the required training; the awareness of the obvious and potential danger; the rules of the road: marked lanes, reflective paint, lane bumpers, rumble strips, signage, warnings, penalties, maintenance and improvements in the roadways; clear goals, objectives, and benefits. The freedom, desire, and necessity of driving are interlaced with responsibility, established by law and mandated by insurance. The element of accountability is accepted and agreed to in order to limit or avoid liability and provide a degree of protection or compensation for damages.

In the realm of communication in general and criticism in particular, there is a vast cavity devoid of required training, skill development, responsibility, or accountability. There is, however, an unmistakable insistence and demand for freedom of speech even if it results in damage ranging from hurt feelings, to demeaning, dehumanizing attacks, fighting, rage, homicide, war, and suicide. Issues such as slander and defamation of character are among a few areas where society has laws to buffer the damage. Otherwise, hundreds of millions of people vie for their right to speak, equipped mainly with the tools and tactics of the win or lose, fight-or-flight mind-set, inherited and developed practices.

Fogging

It is possible to respond to criticism without making things worse using a skill I learned from Dr. Savage referred to as "fogging." The notion behind fogging as a skill is related to driving. When drivers suddenly come upon a bank of fog, most will slow down, turn on their low-beam lights and flashers, and proceed with caution. However, there are reports that a small percentage of people will speed up, intending to quickly get through a fog bank. This is one cause of chain reaction crashes on certain roadways when fog is heavy. We would all do well to slow down in foggy situations and allow adequate distance between vehicles as a preventative measure. Application of the skill of fogging to delicate, sensitive relationship situations is often helpful when responding to criticism, keeping assessment, intention, responsibility, and desired outcome as integral to the plan and action.

The critic's verbal statements are generally preceded by nonverbal expressions. Many behaviors of the critic and critizen are illustrated by drivers. The body and the brain are involved in presenting and responding to criticism. Keen observation of the nonverbal and the verbal data and skillful presentation are very helpful in defusing or diffusing a critic's observation.

Example

An employee—let's call him Ralph—lost objectivity, became emotionally charged, overstepped his bounds, and *inappropriately* asked an administrative assistant if her boss was the right person for the job. After speaking, Ralph realized the huge error due to ignoring all elements of the critizone. This was a huge mistake, a grave violation of a communication concept that says words spoken and actions taken cannot be retrieved. This concept is based on the Miranda warning in law enforcement—"Anything you say can be used against you." Speaking and expressing oneself without regard for the critizone can yield unpleasant results.

A few days later, there was an unplanned encounter between the boss in question and Ralph. When the two met, the posture of the boss spontaneously shifted. The boss's face turned red instantly; his body became rigid, and he spoke in a staccato cadence, saying to Ralph, "I need to talk to you in your office now!" Since Ralph knew what this was about and had assumed that the matter would be revisited in some form at some point, he had already prepared for the likelihood by reviewing the situation. He assessed the situation beginning with his mistake, checked his behavior, feelings, and motives. All of this was part of preparing for the likely confrontation. He reflected on his competence, knowledge, and practice of numerous communication skills in order to respond, *appropriately in this instance,* now that he is being confronted.

The two walked to Ralph's office in silence, which gave him some time to reflect on an earlier situation when the two were in a meeting with a member of his staff. In that situation, when the staff member criticized the boss, the words, tone, and body language of the boss were notably defensive. As the meeting continued in a competitive manner (scoring points using the win-lose/right-wrong approach), Ralph asked that the meeting be concluded with no resolution at that time, because it was clear that the verbal and nonverbal escalation of both parties was building toward a likely crescendo of regrettable magnitude. So, Ralph was quite familiar with this boss's tendency to defend, blame, and raise his voice and assert the authority of his position. However, the boss's reaction toward him in this instance was totally justified. Ralph was out of order by raising the issue with anyone and particularly with the administrative assistant.

Once in the office, Ralph sat down in a chair next to the boss and matched his breathing pattern. Sitting behind the desk—that big barrier of defense—was out of the question; sitting directly across from him would put Ralph directly in his line of sight and provide a "clear" shot at the target on which to project his anger. Ralph waited for the boss to speak. After about forty seconds the boss said, "My administrative assistant informed me that you questioned my fitness for the job, and I am really angry that you would do such a thing."

Ralph said, "I was wrong and out of line in making such a statement. Will you accept my apology? I was completely out of line and am prepared to accept the consequences for my behavior." There was complete silence in the office for about twenty seconds or so.

The boss sat back in the chair, breathing calmly. The tension in his face and body released, his skin tone returned to normal, and then he said, "You know, Ralph, I really appreciate the work you do around here." He cited a few examples of things he appreciated, stood up, shook hands with Ralph, and went on his way.

That is the effect fogging can have on a situation. Had Ralph been argumentative or defensive in an attempt to justify his behavior, prove his point, or protect himself from the criticism, there would likely have been increased tension and anxiety, disagreement, and escalation followed by deterioration of the conversation and perhaps the relationship. Had that happened, there might have been a human resources (HR) situation with

51

a likely write-up, suspension, or other disciplinary action. Instead, the situation was defused.

In addition to or instead of fogging, you can respond to a criticism with a paraphrase, perception check, or creative question. Below are some options in response to a criticism about driving too fast.

1) You're feeling uncomfortable with my driving at this speed.
2) You'd feel better if I slowed down some.
3) Does this speed remind you of a previous unpleasant experience?
4) Are you concerned about the police and a ticket?
5) Would you feel better securing alternative transportation?
6) I guess another ticket would really compromise the budget or result in my license being suspended.

Warning about humor

Laughter (cheerfulness) and fun have a place in life. They can even do good—like a medicine, according to Proverbs 17:22. Just make sure the laughter is not at the expense of any one's self-esteem, dignity, integrity, or life.

Let me share an experience that incorporates several of the basic principles of communication and related skills to come to a mutually beneficial outcome. Other situations will require variations as determined by the situation and the critizone.

Sammy and School

Sammy, an eight-year-old boy, was the object of teasing and ridicule by classmates, and he consequently became resistant to going to school, to the point of dreading the idea. Those doing the teasing experienced no consequence (responsibility or accountability) for their behavior and were actually rewarded by their peers with praise and recognition.

Sammy's parents wanted him to help him so they told him to toughen up, grow "thicker skin," and "not let it affect you." After some period of time spent talking to Sammy, the teacher, and some staff at the school, they experienced only minimal and temporary improvement, and then the same patterns reemerged with more intentional tactics on the part of the perpetrators. Feeling exhausted and disappointed, the parents brought this matter to my attention. I met with them twice and learned enough to propose that I hold a workshop for them and their child with the participants making a commitment to attend and practice with the hope (*likelihood*) that the situation involving their child would change. They suggested that I expand the workshop to other children and their parents. The invitation was extended to other children who were being bullied and teased. The parents were urged (*required*) to attend.

Part I

Step 1: Data Gathering

The workshop was introduced (*the introduction was practiced beforehand*) by Sammy's parents to the group of eight parents, five children, and three older siblings. I facilitated the group and heard from the parents and the children.

After some initial reluctance and awkwardness, the children were encouraged to share their thoughts and feelings openly and freely. (*This was in the format of a modified learning circle*).

As the children began to share their experience, a bond formed among the children and the parents.

Step 2: Communication and Relationships

Next I explained some basics of communication, associated principles and its impact on relationships. I consider these to be universal.

- All relationships are based on communication.
    - There is a distinction between information and communication. Information or data is often one-sided. Communication is an exchange of thoughts, feelings, beliefs, and ideas about experiences. To elucidate, I ask an individual or group to name a famous person, someone likely to be known by lots of people. Athletes, politicians, and entertainers usually top the list. Then I ask them to tell me something about the person: age, education, career, family, how they became famous, their scheduled events and appearances, and even some of their social, political, or religious views. That's information. Chances are the famous person has never talked individually with the person in the group who knows so much about the famous person. There is no exchange of data, thoughts, ideas, or beliefs with the famous person. The point is that many couples, families, and groups, sometimes nations, basically operate on information about each other versus a meaningful

exchange of communication that reveals some of the essence of the person beyond the sound bites.

- The nature of the communication dictates the nature of the relationship. Lousy communication yields a lousy relationship. Communication that is on-again and off-again yields a relationship that is on-again and off-again.

- The person doing the talking is informing the listener as to how best to respond.
This applies in many fields of practice. What the patient says informs the physician about what questions to ask, what tests to run, what remedies to offer or suggest. The auto mechanic learns from the customer what tests to run and what systems to repair in the car. The chef prepares the meal based on what the client desires to eat. The barber and salon operator learn what procedures and styles to perform for the desired cut, shampoo, and hair style from the customer. The listener learns from the speaker how best to respond, even when the speaker criticizes.

- The meaning of what is said is determined by the listener.

- Communication, once conveyed, cannot be retrieved. Words of apology and regret cannot remove the wound that was perpetrated by the spoken word.

- Count the cost of what you are about to say or do, before doing so. Be wary of extended commentary. Urgent or emergency situations have some degree of flexibility on this point.

After discussion on these points, with relevant examples, and a sense that the concepts were understood, the next topic was self-control, which begins with diaphragmatic breathing. Correct breathing happens when the lungs expand, pushing the diaphragm down resulting in the stomach going out. Upon release of the breath, the stomach goes in. Watch newborn babies breathe, take a class in yoga or martial arts, train with a voice coach or teacher, or get a good athletic coach—in these and selected other settings, you will see and experience diaphragmatic breathing. Correct breathing helps you ground and balance yourself, thus reducing your personal and emotional stress load, making more avenues of problem-solving potential and capability more readily accessible and available.

Part II

Step 3: Self-Control—Breathing

Do your own experiment. Breathe diaphragmatically. Get in touch with your feelings and emotions. Notice the communication signals within your body. Learn them. Acknowledge and identify them. This applies to males as well as females. The next time you feel anxious, fearful, angry, giddy, or ecstatic, notice your breathing. Barring an emergency or some urgent situation, breathe intentionally, using your diaphragm. Give yourself a few repetitions and feel the difference. Another test is, if your bladder begins expressing its needs to void—breathe. Lungs expand, diaphragm moves down, and stomach goes out. Breathe intentionally and correctly and bring your body under your control as you make your way to the nearest restroom.

Correct, diaphragmatic breathing is essential to establishing and maintaining control of one's own emotions and self. The only person anyone can control (meaning cooperation and participation—as distinguished from force, manipulation, chicanery) is him- or herself. We may have influence, power, and authority in some settings, yet control comes about through cooperation and participation, not by fiat. The fact of being a parent or boss or holding positions of power doesn't automatically come with "control." Think about nighttime feedings for infants and the like.

Example: If you are driving along in your car and press the brake pedal to slow down, but the pedal goes to the floor, and pumping the pedal doesn't slow the car enough to avoid running the red light and hitting another vehicle. When asked what happened, you might say—truthfully—you lost control. You took the appropriate action, but the car failed to cooperate with the command, and it did not participate with your intention to stop at the light.

Example: If you have fallen asleep and lay on your arm so that the blood circulation is reduced, the pain and feeling of numbness awakens you. There is an instinct to move your arm to get the blood flowing again, and yet the arm is still and feels heavy. For the moment, there is no control. Your thoughts, wishes, and intentions go unheeded until the circulation is restored and you regain control. Then your arm cooperates and participates as desired.

Cooperation and participation on the part of other people in your sphere of influence determines whether there is control, compliance, passive-aggressive issues, and the like.

So, in relationships, cooperation is a goal that can lead toward mutually beneficial outcomes in practically any area of life or endeavor.

Match or Pace

Another breathing practice is to match or pace the other person you are with, whether in the office or courtroom, at home, or on the basketball court, playground, or backyard. Notice the pattern and rhythm of his or her breathing. If you can comfortably do so, match the breath pattern and rhythm of the other person—and notice the dynamics between the two of you. The other person need not know what you are doing. If the other person is breathing at a rate faster than you normally breathe, set up a ratio—say one of your breaths to four of the other person's. This would be pacing. Again, notice the dynamics and the likely movement toward connection—maybe even harmony. If you are with several people, select one person to connect with by matching or pacing that person's breath. That may likely be the speaker or spokesperson. Do this as the individuals take turns speaking. Experiment further by pacing someone who isn't speaking and notice what happens. This is a nonverbal communication experience.

These steps do require some patience and a degree of paradigm shift in the realm of patience. With practice and intention, they can become part of one's unconscious skill set and abilities to have among the options to select from when relationship improvement is a high priority and value.

Step 4

Listening

Once breathe stabilization has occurred, the next step is listening. Here is where concepts, skills, and practices mentioned previously coalesce to help shape and determine the nature of the relationship.

An alert here is worthy of all the attention and focus we can garner. Keen, sensitive, and attentive listening can very likely enhance relationships or perhaps attenuate the tension and friction rather than agitate and amplify. Inattention, unfocused hearing, and stress can result in a competitive experience without even knowing what happened to run things aground.

Please be aware and alert to the reality that 93 percent of our communication is nonverbal. This means that tone and body language make up the bulk of the messages we send and receive. Listening involves all the senses.

The Body Speaks

Your presentation of and response to criticism is comprised of three components: words, tone, and body language. An observation or opinion may be spoken with a tone or body expression that can be interpreted as a criticism, though not intended. An abrupt turn away, a hand gesture, rolling of the eyes, or a deep sigh may be taken by someone as negative communication though there may have been no such intention.

To minimize the miscommunication, practice prior to interactions. Become aware of how you communicate, your idiosyncrasies, tics, and so on. One method is to use the mirror and notice your facial expressions as well as other body posture. Other methods include classes, workshops, and seminars.

In general, when we implement the practices already mentioned and focus on the relationship using the skills of listening, we can get through most situations involving people. And still there are times when walking away may be wise, safe, or best.

Be they friend or foe, ally or aggressor, playmate or bully, the other person is going to give you cues and clues (93 percent nonverbal) as to how best to respond. The key is listening, minimizing commentary, and responding appropriately versus impulsive, ego-driven, and fear-based reactions to score points to win.

While essential training and study in listening often comprises numerous hours of instruction and practice rounds, I will briefly share a few basic elements to assist you as you purpose to seek harmony. These are essential and foundational. Additionally, please pursue follow-up training and skill development.

Lag Time

Your capacity to listen and observe is stated to be at least three times the talking rate of the speaker. Speaking/talking rates are between fifty and one hundred and fifty words per minute. Listening capacity is from one hundred fifty to eight hundred to a thousand words per minute. The difference between the rate of speech of the speaker and the capacity of the listener to listen is called "lag time." This is time you have to listen to what the speaker says and does, gather data from the privileged information that will cue and guide you toward a mutually beneficial response—as he or she speaks, pauses, breathes, reflects, and so on. The listener can then make an appropriate skilled response. Other uses of the lag time, such as listening to your own self-talk; preparing counterarguments or points; making a to-do list; prepare for grocery shopping; remember to make the list of the all the things to bring on the camping trip, and so on, are more likely to create a tit-for-tat type situation and lose the mutually beneficial outcome.

Listening means tuning in to the speaker and capturing both the verbal and nonverbal elements of his or her experience rather than preparing a defense, excuse, justification, counter-story, or other distraction that minimizes or reduces the sharing of their experience.

To enhance your listening skills and ability, during the lag time (while the other person is presenting) repeat silently in your head what the other person is saying and doing, noting his or her body language, which may be out of the other person's conscious awareness. You have ample time to do so and will be provided information for a skilled response. With commitment and practice to improving listening skills, you will discover that you have more than enough time to do this effectively. It does require a paradigm shift in thinking and practice based on relationship development rather than a competitive model that generally prevails in the cultural landscape of many families, communities, organizations, and some countries.

More often than not, the lag time is used to prepare a counter-story, an alternate story, or turn the spotlight onto self rather than listening to the speaker, thus minimizing the potential of harmony among the parties.

Here's a typical example:

Jay shares a painful experience with Adam. Adam responds by sharing a similarly painful experience of his own or of someone he knows. (This is story—counter-story). The two talk past each other with information. They may express best wishes and go on with their agendas for the day. This is representative of many conversations.

Another example is Henry sharing some very good news with Arnold. Instead of silently noting Henry's verbal and nonverbal content, Arnold's lag time is flooded with questions: How did Henry merit such good fortune? Whose back pocket is Henry in? What favors have been exchanged? Furthermore, how come such things never happen to me? Arnold's internal dialogue is basically self-loathing, pitying, and envious. Listening just didn't happen.

In both situations, the lag time is used to compare or contrast one story with another. Thus, the initial speaker's story gets dropped, minimized, or dismissed, and the initial listener either highjacks the spotlight and tells his or her own story; tunes out; or walks away. It's information based and time sensitive, rather than relationship based. Study, learn and practice listening skills to move into the realm of cooperative rather than competitive living.

Another way this could happen is for Adam to briefly restate the essence of what Jay shared and be silent or reflective of the emotional impact this had on Jay, which will likely convey to Jay that Adam was attentive and actually listening thus establishing a link between them on this topic. Adam may have another opportunity to share his similar experience with Jay at another time or with another person at another time. This is using the lag time to effectively listen.

These methods and skills can be taught and demonstrated in our day-to-day conversations at home with our family members. Here the children will learn this method as proficiently as they learn the standard competition based conversations, attitudes, and behaviors.

Part III

Continuing with the workshop with the eight-year-old and other children I mentioned earlier, with the parents support and the agreement of the children, the children and I roleplayed, alternating the role of the bully and the one being bullied. Sammy was the boy in my workshop. The bully's name was Gerald. Both names are fictitious.

> Gerald: Hey, stupid.
> Sammy: Excuse me. Are you talking to me?
> Gerald: Yea! You are so stupid you don't even know when somebody is talking to you.
> Sammy: My name is Sammy. What would you like to talk about?
> Gerald: Don't you get smart with me.
> Sammy: My intention is to have a conversation if you like.
> Gerald: Don't nobody want to talk to you.
> Sammy: In that case, I'll continue on my way.

There were several iterations of this with me and the children switching roles. The parents were invited to join in the role-play and practice intervening engagement with the bully (critic) rather than avoiding, dodging, or fighting back.

As the group committed to meeting, spending time together, and sensing the depth of the emotional and psychological benefits of our joint work, the parents began to self-monitor their interactions with themselves, spouses, children, significant others, coworkers, and others and reported the positive benefits of the changes they were realizing.

In the workshop, Sammy smiled and expressed a level of confidence knowing that he had options to pursue instead of merely cowering. Everyone practiced breathing and reported feeling more in control of their own emotions, less anxious, and less stressed in many situations.

Of course, personal safety is a high value in tense situations. So, if there is evidence or an indication of danger, get help immediately.

****

I have been asked by a number of parents what to do when someone hits or pushes their children. The setting could be daycare, school, home, church, playground, or elsewhere.

My first response is usually to ask what they think? Many will say, "I tell him or her to hit 'em back." The conversation goes along the following line.

> Bill: What is likely to happen when your child hits the other child back?
> Parent: Probably more pushing or hitting.
> Bill: What happens next?
> Parent: Things might escalate into a fight, and maybe others join in on either side of the skirmish.
> Bill: As the skirmish continues, what happens?

There is usually a pause as they contemplate what happens next.

Parent: Someone will get the teacher or find an adult to break things up, or the teacher sees what's happening and intervenes. Then the parents are called to a meeting with the principal, teacher(s), and the children, and the matter is sorted out as best they can.

At this point I ask for permission to do a rework of the situation.
Joe intentionally hits Andrew.

Andrew: Keep your hands to yourself.

Joe comes toward Andrew to hit him again. Andrew goes to get the teacher. The response of many parents is "that's going to make him look weak, like a sissy or tattletale" (name-calling and labeling). To which I reply, since you are going to get the teacher in the first scenario—after the fight—how about going to get the teacher before the fight?

Time for reflection—would you prefer that your child fight rather than switch? Or find another approach and perhaps avoid a fight with all the associated elements of fighting, including but not limited to physical, social, perhaps financial, or legal matters.

Some people have said to me, "We don't talk in situations like this we stand up to it. Talking never solved anything."

My reply: "Either way, both parties will talk at some point. It may be to the teacher, parent, or principal or, in some cases, the lawyer or the judge." It's amazing that people talk after the fight to solve a problem—as if talking in order to prevent or avoid a fight was never an option without fighting first. My message and method is to seek mutually beneficial outcomes and establish harmony. It is possible in most instances. If not, walk away or get help.

In the interest of national security, we are told "If you see something—say something." However, in many local situations in a community, home, at school, at work, in the political or business arena, or on public transportation, if you see someone or a group of people selling or distributing drugs, bullying, harassing, threatening someone, or engaged in some type of questionable or clearly wrong behavior and report it, you may be called and treated as a snitch. Fear often overpowers courage and the contagion grows and spreads.

I propose that we repurpose the awesome power of speech and learn listening skills with the intention of building mutually beneficial relationships. Herein we can reshape our own life and the lives of those we care about and care for. Let this be a new dimension that promotes the freedom of speech coupled with the responsibility of such speech.

Chapter 8

CRITICISM DEFERRED

There was a workplace situation involving two males. One was a jokester (harasser) who had a way of imposing himself onto others—he was a measured or calculating bully. Let's call him Joey.

The other was a very mild mannered, quiet, quite competent, attentive person. Let's call him Paul. Joey knew that he could get under Paul's skin and did so at will with pleasure over an extended period of time. All of Joey's coworkers and others knew about Joey and his antics with Paul in particular but said nothing to Joey or Paul. They did talk to each other about how Joey was getting to Paul and that Paul should stand up to Joey. After nearly two years, on a particular day, the pressure built to the boiling point with Paul. When Joey came with his usual antics, things got physical. Paul reacted in a manner that was contrary to his predictable pattern. The two got into a full-blown fistfight on the job. Now there was intervention on the part of coworkers, who pulled the two apart, separated them, and notified the supervisor and HR after the fight. Both employees were fired.

The company did not tolerate fighting. It was nonnegotiable. Neither did they talk to staff about how to intervene if they saw patterns of behavior that indicated stress and tension or if they witnessed bullying or if they were bullied. The topic could have been addressed in the handbook and other forums. Companies have mandatory training in safety, disaster response, fire drills, and the other in-service training. However, there were no in-service meetings or trainings on the topic of fighting or bullying, nor has any training been provided even after the fight. It's often puzzling that those closest to the situation talked about the numerous episodes of the bullying and now felt bad that the "good guy" was fired along with the bully. They talked about the situation after the fight.

One approach that could have been used was for colleagues to let the bully know which of his antics were unprofessional and unsuitable for the workplace. This would be talking to the person about the situation rather than talking to others about the situation. If he ignored it and continued, the bully would be informed that he would be reported to the supervisor and, if necessary, to HR. Is this snitching? Is this caring enough to act to protect coworkers' employment and livelihood? Are we sometimes content that we aren't the victim (yet), burying our heads in the sand and refusing to see what is right before our eyes? A case of willful blindness. The flow of Dr. Allport's sequence of events shows how ignoring a matter can lead to voicing undesirable consequences after an event that might have been avoided if voiced earlier. See something, say something. The question is when and to whom?

To reiterate, Paul's coworkers all talked about what could or should have happened earlier—after the fight, after the damage is done. Yet no one acted in a preemptive manner. This was a dreadful example of the bystander effect. Is there a situation that you are thinking of now that may warrant your voice?

The challenges and issues associated with seeing something and saying something, being a whistleblower, are often opposed and frowned upon even among professionals, and one can be punished, labeled a snitch, suffer name-calling, isolation, discrimination, physical attack, or be terminated (applying Dr. Allport's understanding) making it easy for many people to keep silent when trouble is staring them in the face, in the bright light of day as well as the shadows of the night. The negative response experienced by many who risk speaking out (who may be labeled as a snitch or whistleblower) can be punishment, isolation, or worse for themselves, their families, and friends. This response is predictably voiced as "mind your own business" even by adults.

The fact that there are whistleblower laws—that may not be enforced—shines light on a deeply embedded culture of life commandments that presents attitudes and practices that have a tendency to promote a culture of nonintervention, or turning a blind eye, prior to a fight or other tragedy. After the tragedy, people "come together" in the aftermath to mourn what might have been avoided.

Who is willing to change in this regard? Proficiency in good communication skills and courage is worthy of consideration.

****

A Workplace Situation Not Deferred

Gina worked for a midsized company with about a thousand employees. The company had a campaign to enhance customer service, and they devised a game to encourage memorization and implementation of the program. All participants would receive a prize for participating as well as other prizes for additional achievements. Gina had several challenges that were difficult to overcome, yet she struggled to memorize the information and received a sash for her initial attempt. Other staff members received the additional prizes, and emblems were attached to their sashes. Gina was encouraged by receiving the sash, though she didn't receive any of the other prizes. Yet, she was eager to work on memorizing the information and receive the prizes at a later date. However, when she appeared before her coworkers with only the sash and no emblems, they began to laugh and joke about how she must be really slow or dumb. These were adults, professionals in their chosen fields of endeavor. Gina was crushed and devastated. Allport's circumlocution element is notable.

One of the program coordinators saw Gina crying as she walked down a hallway. The coordinator approached her, and they found a quiet place as she expressed her sorrow. Upon hearing and seeing her pain, the coordinator offered to intervene on her behalf with the staff. Gina strongly objected, embarrassed that she hadn't done better. Her prior enthusiasm vanished, and she did not want to address the matter with her coworkers. She said she was going to get her personal items and go home. As she entered the elevator, the staff member entered and said to her, "I'm going with you, and together we will talk to the staff." She relented. When they came to her work area, seven of her coworkers were sharing the excitement and fun of the event.

The coordinator politely asked to speak to the group that was assembled and informed them of the impact of their actions on their coworker. Gina was there—crying. Their verbal and nonverbal responses conveyed shock! Apologies were extended, and Gina accepted their apologies. She later told the coordinator that she was glad for the intervention. The hurt, humiliation, and pain of that dreadful experience was ameliorated to some extent by addressing the matter in the present, thus avoiding and carrying the festering sense of shame and embarrassment. And yet it is likely that some amount of negative talk could have continued after the intervention.

Gina's coworkers had no regard for her extenuating circumstances (critizone) as compared to their own. They merely judged her prima facie. Upon seeing that she had no emblems on her sash, when compared to themselves and other staff members, they assumed that she was somehow deserving of being humiliated and degraded, laughed at, and talked about—not even noticing or caring enough to notice her 93 percent nonverbal communication, not realizing that she'd heard them talking about her. This was a case of adding insult to injury. They saw winners and a loser.

> Note: Comparison is helpful in areas such as purchasing goods and services, budgeting, or keeping track of one's personal progress on a variety fronts. It requires a significant paradigm shift to avoid comparing one person to another and calls for distinguishing the individual as other than a product or other item of comparison.

Warning!
The more you carry, the more you weigh.

There are situations where significant matters are minimized for long periods of time—weeks, months, years, even decades. This has the effect of implying acceptance, tolerance, or perhaps comfort with "the way things are" by the perpetrator and the victim. Avoidance to this extent can develop into a breeding ground of contempt, hostility, illness, even murder, or murder/suicide. The concomitant side effects and shelf life can spread beyond the initial parties, last for generations, and become the legacy of a community such as the Hatfields and McCoys.

The Rice Story
During a trip to Oklahoma, I visited a couple in their home. I had met them years earlier prior to their move to Oklahoma. The visit was comparable to earlier visits. During this visit, a variety of topics were discussed, as was usually the case. They were seated beside each other on a love seat, and I was seated diagonally to the man's left. It was a lovely day; the atmosphere was cordial and pleasant. As we talked something was said

that prompted me to make an inquiry of him. The conversation progressed as stated below. Their comments are italicized.

> May I ask you a personal question?
> *Sure, nothing to hide here.*
> Is there something that she does that bugs you?

Pause—he shifts his weight, turns his body away from her and more toward me, crosses his legs, stares off into space, and after a few moments, he speaks.

> *No!*

Taking the cue from his body language (93 percent), seeing the incongruence between his verbal and nonverbal expressions, I surmise that he is being other than candid. Note: this is privileged information, freely presented on his unconscious level, not to be shared with them.

> It may be a small thing, but there is something that really
> gets on your nerves!

Maintaining the aforementioned body posture, after a long pause he speaks again.

> *I hate rice!*

With more volume and intensity, he repeats the statement several times)

> *I hate rice!*

His face is flushed and his eyes glistened with moisture as he says feebly once more)

> *I hate rice!*

His wife promptly puts her hands over her mouth as her head moves backward. Her eyes enlarge, and she looks at him with what can only be described as astonishment.

After a very long period of silence, I sensed changes in the environment and asked him to explain.

The gist of the story follows. Prior to marriage, early in the relationship, she'd offered to cook a meal for him. This had been a very positive indication that things had been going in the desired direction for both of them. He had been excited and optimistic. She had been elated that he'd accepted the offer. Neither of them had discussed a menu—likes, dislikes, allergies, or preferences. After all, they had been in love, happy with each other, and very pleased with the relationship. However, there had been a slight matter that had not been revealed at that meal nor in the early years of the relationship, and it wouldn't be manifest until this visit in their home over thirty years later.

He didn't like rice. He'd never liked rice, no matter who prepared it. It was a food that he'd never cared for since childhood and intentionally avoided. Yet he hadn't revealed this to his beloved at the offer of that meal nor at any meal since that time. Guess what? She hailed from the Caribbean. So, when he'd arrived at her place for that first meal, rice had been the main dish. He'd said nothing, had given no hint that she could detect. We don't know if she might have ignored any hint that may have been present. He may have masked his body language to conceal his dislike of the dish. She may have disregarded any seeming incongruence or missed it altogether. Perhaps in the moment, with his beloved before him, he could have suffered a lapse of memory about his lifelong aversion to rice. Is love blind, afraid, or numb?

At that meal, he'd eaten the rice and the other items with gusto! She'd offered more rice, and he'd eagerly accepted. Since rice had been the main dish, his response had led her to believe, or more correctly to presume, without checking, without verification, that he'd loved rice. So, each time she'd prepared a meal, rice had been there in some form. This hadn't been unusual for her, yet she'd made it with a special sense of love and affection for him. Each time he'd eaten with gusto, though he hadn't liked rice.

Their relationship had advanced through dating to engagement to marriage. All during the marriage she'd prepared rice every day, again, not unusual for her but with special touches for him. Based on her observations and experience from the very first meal, the man had loved rice and perhaps particularly her rice. When the children had joined them, she'd made the same effort to prepare rice for her man, in addition to the duties of the home, motherhood, work, church, and community life.

During this revelatory visit, she'd told of several times during the marriage when she'd come home from a day at work, checked the needs of the children after school, then gone to the kitchen to prepare dinner and discovered she'd been out of rice. She'd altered her initial plan, gathered the children, and gone to the store to buy rice for her man.

Three decades later, in the living room of their home, he came clean. The impact of this revelation may be likened to being shocked when you turn on the radio or like a treadmill that suddenly stops during your running workout. It was very difficult for her to hear that something so much a part of the relationship, and believed to be important and meaningful, was actually hated. This was deeply painful!

When asked the reason for not expressing his dislike of rice early in the relationship, you guessed it. He said, "I didn't want to hurt her feelings." When I asked her how she felt, she said, "I am hurt, confused, and not a little angry. To think I spent all these years making sure I was doing what he wanted, and now to hear that he *hates* rice, is rather confounding and hurtful. It's hard and deeply painful to hear!"

Now she wanted to know from him, "Are you hiding any other thing or things from me"? Such is the risk of criticism deferred. It is very intriguing that he was actually hiding something, though when initially asked about responding to a personal question he said, "Nothing to hide here."

It is highly likely that had he spoken up earlier, even at the first meal, she may have been pleased that he was strong enough and sensitive enough to risk sharing his true feelings and preference.

The longer criticism is deferred, the more intense the impact when the revelation is presented, the more hurtful to the recipient, the higher the cost! It is difficult to know or calculate the type and degree of emotions he carried for over thirty years. It was crystal clear at the disclosure that he was upset and angry (perhaps at himself), and the intensity of her hurt and disappointment upon hearing this truth.

A redo of this experience could take several forms.

1) At the initial invitation, he could have expressed genuine gratitude and delight and asked permission to share his dislike of rice. Even if she said, "You'll like my rice," at least the matter would have been addressed, very likely without a severe negative impact.

2) He could have agreed to at least taste her rice and share that he still had a dislike of that food, as distinguished from her rice. Now she would know that even her rice was still rice to him. Hopefully, she would accept his revelation, still pursue the relationship, and cook other foods.
3) She could have inquired about his likes, dislikes, or preferences from the outset.
4) He could have kept it quiet until he arrived for the meal and, upon seeing the rice, gently and delicately shared his issue.
5) He could have tasted the rice and then made his issue known.
6) She might have asked him what he liked about the meal and if there was anything he'd rather not have at subsequent meals.

These are six options. There are more that could be used, depending up the nature of the situation and the personalities involved. Something along this line would have allowed the truth to be presented and avoided thirty years of pretense, ambiguity and pain on his part and utter dismay on hers at the revelation.

As it turned out, two people endured over thirty years of anguish, one not even knowing it, due to that four-letter word that starts with *F* that paralyzed the one who held the secret. Now that the truth was revealed, he was freed from carrying this three-decade-old burden of hiding and pretending. He no longer needed to fear that she would find out. This freedom necessarily led him to address the matter of deception and make major amends for the love and care she put into her provisions for him relative to this matter.

One consequence he now had to bear was her almost certain desire to revisit her question and desire to know if he had hidden other things from her. We had a few follow-up phone visits (before Skype) to address her anger and hurt due to his lack of openness as well as his fear that served as his justification to mislead her. Their love and commitment were reaffirmed in the end. Other couples who hid or pretended for various periods to time didn't fare as well.

It is imperative to know that corrective actions can be made and will very likely require some type of interaction. The interaction need not be hostile, vindictive, or unnecessarily confrontational, though that may be so. It can be healthy, helpful, respectful, and beneficial though painful. Different points of view, beliefs, attitudes, and mistakes can be discussed and resolved among adults and even children, without resorting to verbal attacks or violence as the preferred, automatic default option. Denial or avoidance guarantees an extended shelf life, and the matter can live on with renewed freshness. In some instances, these matters may never be addressed, thus never be resolved. Unresolved matters often fester and burrow into the mind, body, and spirit, affecting one's health, attitude, and outlook on life, sometime setting up barriers, accompanied by embellishments and other hurdles that may interfere with relationships in ways that aren't always obvious. See "The Pinch Package" below.

Pinch Package

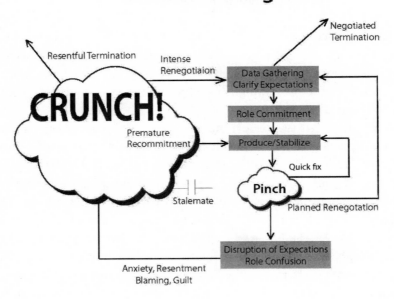

****

The Pinch Package

The Pinch Package is a concept initially designed for use in the workplace. I have found it to be very applicable for use in the home, school, workplace, church, community, and social situations. It offers a very good understanding of how relationships are formed (well or poorly) and the associated dynamics and breakdown of relationships when observations, feelings, and expectations are ignored or minimized, and avoided in an attempt to "keep the peace," "not cause trouble," "not rock the boat," or other scapegoats.

The Pinch Package is sometimes referred to as the Planned Renegotiation Pinch Package, developed by John J. Sherwood and John C. Glidewell (1973, 1975) and extended by John Sherwood and John Scherer, a former naval officer, Lutheran minister, founder of Scherer Leadership International, and author of *Facing the Tiger*. The model is based on the premise that relationships in a social system—be they that of an individual, a pair, a group, an organization, business, or community—seldom proceed as planned or expected. The model describes how social systems are established and become stabilized so work can be done and goals achieved, and how change can enter the system. I first heard of John Scherer from Dr. Savage. I have modified the original diagram slightly.

At times, in some relationships, meaningful data may be withheld, not presented or requested for lots of reasons based on the critizone: time, context, need to know, trust levels, manipulation, nature of the relationship (family, business, political, religious), and fear (refer to the rice story in the previous chapter). In addition to data sometimes being withheld or forgotten, very often expectations are unclear or sometimes ambiguous. Instead of clarifying expectations, people may assume they understand and proceed as if things were clear. Perceptions, misperceptions, and presuppositions can generate feelings of fear, anticipated loss, and confusion. Fear that the truth will be revealed or other fears (real or neurotic) can inhibit the pursuit and clarity of expectations (the rice story). Some people would rather play the you-should-have-known-what-I-was-thinking game rather than speaking openly, honestly, or truthfully. This is often true regarding a criticism or observation that a person is fearful of presenting for any number of reasons—some stated earlier in this book.

Clarity of expectations and motives prove helpful in building, maintaining, and strengthening relationships. Clarification of expectations is encouraged to minimize and perhaps avoid misunderstandings; it helps us drop the you-should-have-known-what-I-was-thinking scapegoat option and address facts and feelings more openly with appropriate caution. The refusal or fear to speak clearly, forthrightly, and sensitively often drives people to live with unmet and unspoken expectations for years or decades. This is too often the case in many marriages and sometimes in employment.

When something goes awry (pinch), as is bound to happen, according to the Pinch Package, there are three response routes:

Number 1 is a *quick fix*. This might be the repair of a flat tire that disrupted the morning carpool. With the tire repaired and follow-up communication to carpool members, things are back on track for the trip back home in the evening. The inconvenience of that morning commute doesn't warrant a change of the initial plan.

Number 2 is a *planned renegotiation*. This response calls for updated information, with a long-term or short-term modification. For a carpool, this might mean two weeks of alternate arrangements while the engine or transmission is rebuilt. It could mean temporary relocation for a few days in the summer time when the home air conditioning system is repaired or replaced.

We altered our life routine during the snowstorm of 2010 when the electricity went out for five days. The house was unbearably cold, so we moved in with our daughter and son-in-law until electricity was restored at our house. Staying with the first two response routes—the quick fix and the planned renegotiation—generally means better relationships, improved trust, prompt response to issues, and harmony among parties.

Number 3 is the *disruption,* which occurs as a result of accumulated pinches that have been ignored, overlooked, excused, justified, or tolerated over time. At some point, the person being pinched gets mad and isn't going to take it anymore. When the disruption occurs, it is followed by four possible routes that lead to the *crunch.* From the crunch the various options are the following:

1) A resentful, sometimes destructive or violent termination occurs, such as an administrative assistant who has been taken for granted for years, not recognized and passed over for promotions that were given to others whom she had trained. One day before a big meeting, she is reminded of the data files, copies, folders, beverages, and snacks needed for all the participants who will arrive from several cities the next morning. She assures her boss and others that she will stay late (which she has done at other times) and have everything ready for the morning meeting. After everyone leaves the office, she lingers for a while, turns off the light, and leaves without doing the work. She leaves never to return. She intentionally left them in a lurch. She feels justified and a degree of satisfaction for the "abusive" treatment that she endured for way too long. Others have done something similar in

settings and situations at home, work, community, organizations, or nations. Some have even refused to accept the final check issued to them; some went into witness protection, and others have gone into exile. Another example is putting a person's goods on the curb and changing the locks on the door without notification. Murder/suicide, while extreme, is another example.

2) A second option from the crunch is the dead end (stalemate), sometimes endured for decades or even generations. I recall a situation in a particular congregation where members of two different families had a bitter argument over a matter. Each side became so acrimonious that they made members of their respective families take an oath not to attend any church function if one member of the other family was present. Anyone from either family that was the first to arrive spotted the car of anyone from the other family would stay away and alert their respective family members. This was before there were cell phones. That practice extended to at least three generations in that congregation.

Sometimes children and adults declare that if their sibling/child/partner doesn't take out the trash, then they aren't either. Other matters include washing the dishes, changing the baby's diaper, paying the bills, getting gas in the car, and so on.

3) A premature recommitment is a response to the crunch. I find this may last for two weeks. For instance, a couple who has had a serious argument and avoided each other for a couple of weeks become lonely and sad enough to want to "put this behind them and move on." They want to go back to the way things used to be before the crunch. So, they "bury the hatchet and make up," without addressing the causes of the problem. The problem will likely reappear with deeper hurt and pain.

4) The fourth response to the crunch is an intense, painful confrontation, usually requiring a mediator or other third party. This could result in an agreed-upon termination or an acceptably beneficial resolution where new data is gathered with clarification, with detailed expectations, and the relationship continues, this time with all parties paying attention to the pinches that will occur and stay in the quick-fix or planned-renegotiation operational modes.

Labor disputes often go through this experience in order to come to terms that both sides can support. Contested divorce situations as well as social or civil unrest in communities sometimes have these experiences as do political campaigns. On an international scale, peace treaties between warring factions or nations may be in this category.

A pinch can be a criticism or become a criticism. Use the information, concepts, and practices in this book to skillfully, successfully navigate the ebb and flow of relationships. Your doing so opens the door and may lead the way to a greater likelihood of a mutually beneficial experience. Address the pinches before they become toxic, costly, and time consuming. Criticisms that are ignored or tolerated can lead to a disruption of a relationship that can lead to a *crunch*. Recovery can be very time consuming and costly.

It is imperative to be appropriately honest (guard and check cues to know what and how much to reveal) in these types of experiences. Assess and evaluate. There are times when another opinion from someone who is neutral can be helpful in developing a plan of action to prevent emotional and psychological issues from becoming wounds that develop scar tissue and calluses.

Think how much further along the pathway of human development we could be socially, politically, financially, environmentally, psychologically, spiritually, and more—if more people had the courage and skill to speak up and make much needed changes that matter greatly in the realm of communication and relationships.

Who might you be if you would be who you could be?
—Unknown

From Observer to Action

Be alert to times and situations when action is called for. The following scenario emphasizes the need to move from observer and wishful thinker to taking action as warranted.

We are passengers traveling on a touring coach. Along the way, you notice that the driver appears to be dozing at the wheel. He nods and bobs his head in ways that indicate he is compromised in his ability to drive. The bus is weaving, and the tires occasionally hit the rumble strips. Other drivers blow their horn to alert the bus driver of danger (a type of criticism). The driver is momentarily roused to attention and yet is still only partially alert, and he drifts back to sleep.

What do you do? Do you start telling other people about the dozing driver? Do they in turn tell others, perhaps call loved ones on their cell phones and tell them? You acknowledge that you and others are passengers and not professional commercial drivers' license (CDL) drivers. Do you go up to the driver and quietly call his/her name, inquiring about the need to stop the bus? Do you get a couple of other passengers to assist with taking control of the coach by removing the driver's foot from the accelerator, hold his arm if needed, remove the driver from the seat if need be, while someone else steers and begins slowing the vehicle?

Or do you remain seated, wishing, hoping, praying, and wait until the coach crashes, hits other vehicles, flips over, landing on its side and burst into flames, and then wait for emergency vehicles and personnel to risk their lives to rescue the injured and recover the bodies of the dead?

There were two different occasions where we were traveling on a motor coach during a time when the weather was cold. On both occasions, it seemed perfectly clear that others on the bus must be cold. They were murmuring. It was easy to see the frost caused by the clash of the heat from our mouths and the cold air. They were wrapped in layers of coats, sweaters and jackets. I waited to see who would go to talk to the driver. And behold, no one went to talk to the driver about the temperature on the bus. It seems that sometimes my purpose is to take the initiative and act on behalf of myself, my wife and others. So, I went repeatedly on both occasions and talked to the driver.

Are you plagued with memories of the way things might have been had you spoke up or acted sooner regarding the bus situation? Do you spend much of your remaining life, "shoulding" all over yourself, going to therapy, talking about what could have been a different outcome if you or someone had risked taking action earlier with the intent to assure the safety of yourself and others on the coach as well as others in their vehicles and avoid the extensive property damage and lawsuits?

The previous stories are examples of how being content, wishful, or fearful observers can generate potentially damaging situations who waited until **after** the damage to **talk** about what might have been. These stories can serve as warnings to help people cease and desist the teasing, kidding, and joking; be the neutral observer; and become empowered people to overcome fear and act to prevent danger when they can.

Help them, and when appropriate, everyone can reflect with smiles, laughter, and tears together rather than weeping and reeling at bedsides, rehab centers, prisons, funerals, and memorials from the carnage inflicted upon individuals, families, and communities who reached a deadly tipping point. Spare yourselves from being overwhelmed with a future of guilt and remorse that can lead to despair, depression, and associated debilitating forms of behavior. Act!

Learn to present criticism appropriately with respect and skill as an agent of healing, help, growth, and maturity. Doing so will enhance the quality of life for yourself, those you love and care about, those you work with, and even for those who may not like you or who may not care for you. Learning, practicing, and implementing specific skills relative to criticism and the spirit of genuine care for the well-being of others and discover that criticism, like nitroglycerin, can be appropriately measured and administered yielding improvements for all.

Since parents are generally the child's first teacher, it is important that we be aware of the likely impact of our verbal and nonverbal messages to the child. Be curious as to how you think the child might be perceiving what is said and the manner in which it is said.

Children cry! There are a variety of reasons that prompt them to cry. Is it possible that a child might feel devalued if someone speaks in a raised voice, while frowning as they say, "Why don't you stop crying"? Could the words and manner of speaking be perceived as a threat or a criticism? Or is this the introduction of a style of communication that the child will learn to interpret, perceive and respond to in a healthy or not so healthy way?

Some toddlers are encouraged as they begin to smile, coo, sit up, attempt to stand, flip over, crawl, fall, walk, run, skip, hop, and jump. Gentle use of appropriate words and nonverbal expressions can provide assurance without wounding. This continues as the child progresses to speaking, reading, writing, coloring, playing, and sharing. Nearly all phases, stages, and interactions in life can be enhanced, even enriched by an observation or criticism—improvement oriented—regardless of the age of the citizen. Material in this book can be used in most situations for interactions where an observation or criticism would likely be beneficial.

So, parents, teachers, and others who work with children, youth, young adults, and adults, be mindful that your communication—verbal and nonverbal—criticism, and judgment may influence the direction one takes in life.

My personal experience—like everyone's—was shaped and fashioned by the inheritance of time and place, a survival mind-set and mentality dominated the landscape of existence (survival of the fittest). Imposed obedience and compliance were the order of the day. Teaching, thinking, and questioning were bitterly opposed and not acceptable. Practically everything was done—in the family, community, social, educational, work, even medical, religious, and political systems—for the purpose maintaining and supporting the status quo. There was no thought or consideration of a need to learn and know about communication skills and relationship formation. What was expected was basically yes and no, compliance and obedience with the established order.

My lack of awareness, understanding, and preparation for the vast array of communication issues related to criticism thwarted my early growth and postponed some aspects of my development. My family and community provided for and protected me according to the custom and culture of the times. However, there were no explanations or instructions about the nature of the world in time and place, leaving me confused and questioning my own sense of worth, value, and being.

By my fortieth year of life, after broader exposure to a larger world, some careful probing, questioning, observation, historical background and setting, and gleanings from family members, community, and nation, I came to understand that I was loved, provided for, and protected in accordance with the goal of survival, not on a relationship basis.

Having learned lessons about the nature and value of these influences— time and place—whether intentional or not—I share with you the imperative of teaching and modeling these critical communication skills to empower those in your sphere of influence so they have options to consider about how they will use their allotment of time, energy, talents, and skills. My prayer is they will move in the direction of harmony and contribute to a better world. It begins at home.

Just as we possess the capacity to learn numerous languages of the peoples on the planet, so too can we learn to communicate in peaceful ways, just as we learn not to be so peaceful.

At this point in my journey I want to encourage and perhaps challenge us to experience the benefits of criticism and repurpose it as an intention toward improvement orientation and embrace the idea that criticism can be a gift.

Alert!

It's time for an upgrade relative to the nature, attitude, culture, and interactions regarding reckless criticism, teasing, joking, and kidding around. The upgrade is to include responsibility for the use of one's words and their power.

Here are a few texts that provide critical alerts or warnings relative to the words we speak. I find these to be applicable to all demographic groups.

> There is one whose rash words are like sword thrusts, but the tongue of the wise brings healing.
> —Proverbs 12:18 KJV

> A soft answer turns away wrath, but a harsh word stirs up anger.
> —Proverbs 15:1 KJV

> Wounds from a friend can be trusted, but an enemy multiplies kisses.
> —Proverbs 27:6 KJV

> Set a guard over my mouth, O Lord, keep watch over the door of my lips.
> —Psalms 141:3 KJV

> Good sense makes a man slow to anger, and it is his glory to overlook an offense.
> —Proverbs 19:11 KJV

> A word fitly spoken is like apples of gold in a setting of silver.
> —Proverbs 25:11 KJV

> When words are many, transgression is not lacking, but he who restrains his tongue is prudent.
> —Proverbs 10:19 KJV

If anyone thinks he is religious, and does not bridle his tongue, but deceives his heart. This man's religion is vain.
—James 1:26 KJV

Death and life are in the power of the tongue, and those who love it will eat its fruit.
—Proverbs 18:21 KJV

The subsequent chapter will lay out the specifics of preparing, presenting and responding to criticism.

Having shared an introduction and some background of my journey into the realm of relationships and criticism, accompanied by an overview of the learning process, let us turn our attention to the elements of context and environment as we repurpose our launch into presenting and responding to criticism 2.0. The information contained in the context and environment is significant in preparing for a criticism either as critic or critizen. The next chapter is making the assessment of the critizone.

Chapter 9

ASSESSMENT OF THE CRITIZONE—PART I

Structure

> Let the first impulse pass, wait for the second.
> —Baltasar Gracian

Assessment of the critizone involves taking into account the pertinent factors that comprise the critical situation.

Ten factors are listed below to help the critic and the citizen in their respective and changeable roles to prepare, present, and respond to criticism for mutually beneficial outcomes. Evaluation of the associated factors for the situation you face is highly recommended before acting in either role. Feel free to amend or modify these factors based on your situation, skill, and support system.

1) Plan.
   Design or determine the nature and accuracy of the criticism prior to presentation or response.

   Note: Many emergency response situations are planned in advance with the intention of minimizing panic, harm, and loss when possible scenarios are thought out in advance, for instance, emergency exits from buildings, aircraft, or ships; disaster preparedness; and more. We note that every commercial airplane flight includes the safety demo or video. I have never seen or heard of a flight crew opting out of presenting the video or demonstration. Perhaps all the passengers "know the drill," and no one has ever become agitated to the point of saying, "We've heard all this before. Can you just get on with the taxiing and takeoff?" It's elementary and an essential part of a flight plan.

Buildings—both commercial and residential, where we live, work, play, pray, socialize, study, and so on, are designed, built, and maintained using plans. This is critical and crucial.

Is it true? (Verifiable)
If true, determine the degree of accuracy.

Example: The supervisor's write-up to HR said the employee is always late. HR determined that the employee was five minutes late one day in the past three months.

If false—inquire about the possible reason(s) and timing for the criticism. Is there misinformation? Is there malicious intent? You can opt to ignore it if that seems best for the desired outcome on your part. Yet not as an avoidance tactic or strategy. If there is hearsay or gossip that warrants a response, you have the options of addressing the matter as gossip, or appropriately encouraging the gossiper to make a direct presentation to the citizen. It is amazing how many gossipers will talk to everyone except the subject of their gossip. Occasionally a critic may opt out of making a criticism based on the information derived from the plan.

2) Who is the critic? Boss, coworker, opponent, subordinate, spouse, child, relative, neighbor, stranger, passerby, associate, acquaintance, friend, public figure?
3) Who is the critizen? Boss, coworker, opponent, subordinate, spouse, child, relative, neighbor, stranger, passerby, associate, acquaintance, friend, public figure?
4) What are the relationship dynamics? Professional, social, family, casual, temporary, ongoing, close, distant, inimical/hostile, legal, political, religious, personal, financial, and so on, positive or negative.
5) What is the motive or intent?
   o   To improve or help

- o To hurt
- o To get even
- o To embarrass, humiliate
- o Revenge
- o Power/manipulation
- o Attention

6) What is the context? Place, time, setting? In public, at the office, home, party, dinner, restaurant, driving, phone, text, email, graffiti, letter in the mail? Is it a competitive venue or situation?

7) Timing and delivery—when are you thinking of presenting the criticism or the response? Is this an anniversary, birthday, significant date or place to either party?
- o Is this a current matter?
- o What is the likely shelf life?
- o Determine if the matter is too old to actually bring up. Listen to your gut. It is helpful to assess or evaluate the information based on the input from your head, heart and gut.

8) Intensity or impact of the criticism (triage)

Level 1—No impact—especially if it's not true. Even if not true, there can be a shadow cast over the critizen. It might be interesting or even helpful to know what prompted the criticism.

Response options:
- ▪ Ignore.
- ▪ Inquire about the reason and timing for this criticism.
- ▪ Respond with facts, then feelings if warranted.
- ▪ If you feel or are wronged, or injured even by the false criticism or allegation, you may want to seek assistance to address the matter.
- ▪ Seek appropriate remedy.
- ▪ Avoid arguing and debate.

Level 2—Negligible

Response options:
- • Weigh the consequences.
- • Ignore.
- • Respond with facts and feelings.
- • Offer a correction if warranted (Follow up appropriately).

Level 3—Mild

Response options:

- Appropriately acknowledge the facts, own your actions.
- Apologize if deemed appropriate.
- Offer to correct the problem. (If such an offer is made, follow through is to be expected.)

Level 4— Significant

Response Options:

- Appropriately acknowledge the facts; own your actions.
- Apologize.
- Offer to correct the problem.
- Accept consequences.
- Seek appropriate help.

Level 5—Crisis

Response Options:

- Acknowledge the facts.
- Own your actions.
- Apologize.
- Offer to correct the problem.
- Ask for forgiveness.
- Provide restitution, compensation or reparations.
- Accept consequences and seek appropriate help.

Level 6—Disaster

Response Options:

- Appropriately acknowledge the facts.
- Own your actions.
- Apologize.
- Offer to correct the problem.
- Ask for forgiveness.
- Provide restitution, compensation or reparations.
- Accept consequences and seek appropriate help.

9) Shelf life. How long has it been since the situation occurred? How long might the actual presentation or response be remembered and carried? Expiration dates range from short-term to indefinite.

10) Options. Select at least six ways to present or respond (even more for those who are adventurous) to the particular criticism and the context.

Options
Disregard or avoid
Ignore
Present with tact and diplomacy
Respond with tact and diplomacy
Reject
Respond in kind
Respond with exaggeration/embellishment
Acknowledge the facts as they are or as best as you can perceive them.
Agree when the criticism is true. If you agree—clearly specify what you are acknowledging.
Example:

> Critic: Your speech was terrible, poorly constructed and presented and lasted for fifty minutes instead of forty-five as agreed upon.
>
> Critizen: I did speak longer that forty-five minutes.

Accept responsibility for what was done, or not done, and accept the consequences of your actions.
Thank the person for their candor.
Apologize—specify what you are apologizing for (Merely saying, "I'm sorry" is inadequate. "Sorry" is to be used when there is nothing you can do or could have done.)

> For instance, I am sorry that the tree fell on your house. I had nothing to do with the tree falling on the house, now that I know what has happened my response is to offer some aid or support. Otherwise based on the song by the Temptations—"Sorry is a sorry word."

Act to correct or mend any damage done.

Having multiple options gives the critic and the critizen flexibility to act and respond without being locked into a predictable default pattern. This flexibility also enables you to count the cost!

Each person is responsible for his or her own actions. Both the critic and the critizen are to make the best presentation and response each can. Taking into consideration all the pertinent elements of the critizone is an excellent way to prepare before presenting or responding to a criticism, experience minimal or no regret and seek a potentially mutually beneficial outcome.

As you think about presenting and responding, be mindful that there is a cost associated with each action or inaction. Weigh the potential costs. Often this factor is ignored, and the emotional trigger is pulled either in presenting or responding, or both with no regard or responsibility for the cost or impact. Such behavior and habit patterns can leave a person or group with little or nothing to buffer the emotional impulse and its damage. So please count the cost.

Chapter 10
ASSESSMENT OF THE CRITIZONE—PART II

Implementation

There are at least two sides to everything: heads and tails; right and left; up and down; inside and outside. Notice the conjunction "and" that relates one side or feature to the other. Both exist at the same time. When it comes to decisions or choices, selecting one "or" the other doesn't eliminate the existence of the other.

In the realm of criticism, the critizone is the environment or context in which both the critic and the citizen exist at the same time. The critic or observer is encouraged to make an assessment of a criticism before presenting it as referenced in the previous chapter. It is equally helpful for the citizen to assess the situation before responding. Assessment considers the critizone (essential elements or factors that constitute the situation) *before* any action is taken by the critic or the citizen. The assessment provides information that can be vital in bringing about the best presentation, best response and best resolution for the best outcome of a criticism.

I'll illustrate the matter of assessment for both parties through a story about two physicians—James and Dale who work in the emergency department of a hospital. Over a period, Dale observed a peculiar pattern of behavior by a number of staff members in their attitudes toward James, a model physician, highly regarded for his skill, knowledge, insight, intuition, and perception. It became clear to Dale that many of the staff were subtly yet increasingly avoiding James and minimizing their interactions with him. Dale didn't know any particular reason for the staff's behavior and wanted to avoid arousing any suspicions or generating any gossip by prematurely asking questions related to his own perception of their behavior. So, he implemented a *plan* to gather data—nonverbal as well as verbal through quiet observation, using the elements of the critizone to make his assessment. Information gathered in this manner in the communication world is sometimes referred to as privileged, akin to the cards in your hand dealt to you when playing a card game. This is not the same as legally privileged information between client and professional. This privileged communication information is revealed unconsciously by the speaker(s), is noted by the observer, and is most often kept to oneself by the observer. There may be instances where it is beneficial or necessary to judiciously make someone aware of his or her unconscious behavior. Prudence is called for in such instances to avoid making an attack or assault on those not conscious of the behavior.

On a particular day, Dale finds a probable basis for the behavior in question during a meeting at the nurses' station. As James gave directions about a particular patient to the staff, two nurses waved their hands in front of their faces and rolled their eyes as he spoke directly to them. Dale deduced that James had a strong case of halitosis, and no one on the staff had told James. This *must* have been the reason for their odd behavior, he surmised! Making full use of the critizone, Dale staged several close encounters with James and found his suspicions profoundly substantiated. James had bad breath! Now that he had the necessary information, Dale was faced with the challenge of *how* to tell his coworker and dear friend about the problem and keep their relationships intact.

Dale presumed that it was very likely James had lost most, if not all, of his sense of smell and, thus, probably didn't know that his breath was offensive. James may have likely been so focused on his work that he was oblivious to the obvious, not-so-subtle signals around him, or he shrugged off the signals, attributing them to "the way some people are." It was clear to Dale that James's bad breath was fast becoming iconic. Considering another element of the critizone, Dale curiously wonders if James's wife knew about the matter. Had she told him? If so, how could he ignore her? If not, what might have been her reasons for not saying anything to him about it, or was she likewise olfactory challenged? In order to avoid spending countless moments in perpetual conjecture filling in blanks, Dale simply decided that he would present the matter to James and tell him about the bad breath.

After a bit of pondering and contemplation as to how, when, and where to break the news, elements of the critizone, Dale decided to present his criticism and observation using the model of triage in the emergency department (ED) to help get his message across and hold both James's and his relationship and self-esteems intact. He used triage because it was familiar to both of them and likely easy to relate to and make the application.

Dale suggested that he and James have lunch on one of their days off, when neither was on call. James was grateful for the offer and looked forward to having lunch with his friend.

On the appointed day, the lunch experience was pleasant and enjoyable. The two discussed topics of family, school reunions, politics, the economy, gadgets, and the like. Work was not discussed at all. After dessert, Dale asked permission to change the direction of the conversation. The dialogue went as follows, with my commentary in parentheses.

Dale: James, I'd like to discuss a personal matter with you. Is that okay?

(This approach acknowledges both parties, seeks permission, and waits for the go ahead—or not—before launching into the delicate matter or situation. If the answer is no, honor the response and wait, ask for a more appropriate occasion, or use other skills to get a yes.

James senses that something is amiss and displays a bit of caution, if not suspicion, for the whole lunch meeting.)

James: What's this about? Does this have something to do with work?

Dale: It's a personal matter that likely has some ramifications at work.

(He asks again in a gentle, soft tone)

Is it okay to discuss a personal matter?

(James reluctantly agrees to the discussion based on their friendship and good history—critizone. Dale hears and feels the go ahead.)

Dale: Since we both work in the ED, I would like to ask you to triage the issue I am about to bring to your attention.

James: Triage?

Dale: Yes, triage. Use the best model of triage for the best outcome of a given ED situation and apply it to the matter I am going to present to you.

James: So, you have some emergency situation to talk about?

Dale: Emergency is too strong. But it is a matter that I would like to bring up, and I am certain that a positive outcome is achievable.

(James agrees with an awareness of the butterflies he felt in his stomach—his enteric nervous system—sometimes referred to as the "brain of the gut." The cautious consent was based on their relationship. He then reflected on various triage situations, contexts and rating systems.)

(*Triage* is the determination of properties for action in a medical emergency. Patients are prioritized for treatment according to the seriousness of their conditions or injuries, the skills of the staff, and the capacities of the facilities. This allows for the consideration of various options in order to ensure the most appropriate response for the best outcome. For those who may not be familiar with triage, you will find a list of some of the rating systems in the appendix. I strongly recommend this approach or some type of assessment to agree on for the critic and the citizen before presenting or responding to a criticism. Weather alert/information is a model that can be used as well as numerous others.)

(Criticism, like all situations, occur in various settings and circumstances, and it has a shelf life. Like medical emergencies, people who are criticized and those presenting a criticism will display physical signs of discomfort. Some signs are increased pulse rate, elevated blood pressure, changes in respiration, perspiration, skin color variations, dilated pupils, and shifts in posture. Using the triage model and levels best suited for a particular situation can assure the best presentation, best response, and best outcome to a criticism.)

(Keep in mind that some outcomes may be difficult, painful, and perhaps disappointing. While these may not be desirable, the criticism can still be presented in order to avoid neglect due to fear, and later regret.)

(Now Dale and James are on the same page.)

Dale: James, I just want to tell you that I detect you have a very strong case of halitosis.

(Dale appropriately pauses, and after gauging that James is expressing some degree of discomfort, yet isn't defensive, he continues.)

I am sharing this information with you based on my own awareness of the problem. Further, it may well be affecting at least some of the staff's reactions or responses in the ED.

(Dale pauses, and waits—wait training—for a reply from James. After a few moments of silence)

James: You want me to triage your statement?

Dale: My statement could be regarded as a criticism by some people. I am hopeful that your skill in triaging my statement or criticism will prove beneficial.

James: Well, I can see that this approach is helpful and acceptably different. While I was cautious, even suspicious as to what you were up to, I am greatly relieved.

(Brief pause)

So then, the initial assessment finds that I am hopelessly deficient in smelling—even myself! That's because my olfactory system is completely nonfunctioning and in need of a "new factory!" I can hardly ever detect any smells, odors, or fragrances. You say that you are sharing this based on your own awareness?

Dale: Yes, I wanted to know for myself and help if I could.

Consider two quotes:

> I love you, and because I love you, I would sooner have you hate me for telling you the truth than adore me for telling you lies.
>
> —Pietro Aretino

> Criticism and dissent are the indispensable antidote to major delusions.
>
> —Alan Barth

James: Well, this is awkward and clumsy. Embarrassing!

(After a long silence)

I sincerely thank you, Dale. You are truly a friend. I feel embarrassed, humbled, and yet honored that you approached me directly and in such a caring and skillful way—like a surgeon.

I have known about this for some time and chose to ignore it, though there have been many indications that something might need attention. I suppose now is the time to face the music and address the matter.

True confession...

(Long pause)

Actually, my wife, Kathy told me many times that I should see a doctor about the breath situation. I ignored her and in a way put her down. It appears that she just quit telling me after a while, though she likely couldn't ignore it herself—or worse, tolerated it! Oh my, this is really painful on many fronts.

(Long pause)

As I ponder this matter, I can see how some of the staff reactions to me are very likely related to my bad breath, and not things I have imagined

90

and dismissed as justification for my denial of this problem. I denied that the problem might be with me.

(Sigh)

So, I'll see a doctor this week, get a second opinion, and get this matter under control as best I can. When I get home today, I'll face Kathy, or perhaps I won't face her. Well, I could make sure I brush my teeth and use a mint before facing her. Nonetheless, I will acknowledge my error, maybe even arrogance, to Kathy and apologize for my cocky, insensitive attitude and the harsh things I have said to her about this. I will also talk to the staff. Hmm, I wonder if any patients have been offended by the bad breath. Oh my, I've got some work to do. Thank you again, Dale. The time has come for me to acknowledge this matter, and I do so! I will buy some breath mints on our way out of here.

****

The benefits of considering and assessing the critizone in presenting and responding to criticism using some type of assessment that addresses both sides of the situation is a preferred approach that has better chances for an amicable resolution. It allows for a measured response based on facts and feelings that are as objective as the parties are willing to be. Other professions and occupations use tools of assessment in presentation and response. Automotive repair (electrical, transmission, engine); physical therapy; dental care; news and information services; meteorology; finance, police situations; hair stylists; National Transportation Safety Board (NTSB); rescue situations; nuclear testing and sensors for weapons; and boundless other lines of work rely heavily on tools and methods of assessment to determine the problem and the appropriate response for the best outcome. In addition to the technical elements of assessment, often family, friends, medical, and social histories play a vital role in presenting information, and when responding to a situation. These are elements of the critizone.

A Hit-and-Run Situation

A family member, let's call her Emma, is visiting her relative in a healthcare facility in the Midwest. This is a daily practice and has been for several years. She visits and helps care for her aunt, and she also assists others, especially at mealtimes. On a particular day, during the lunch period, an administrator passed through the area and spoke to Emma across the room. "You haven't attended the feeding class, so you can't help feed anyone until you do." Everyone in the area heard the admonition, including other staff and at least one other family member. Emma was embarrassed and felt deep shame and humiliation. The administrator continued on her way, oblivious to any emotional impact as she publicly conveyed the facts.

About five weeks later. Emma conveyed this event to another staff member—let's call her Janice. As she recounted the details, Emma's facial expressions portrayed the gravity of the situation for her. With very animated gestures, misty eyes, and a trembling voice she said, "I must have told a thousand people about this."

"A thousand?" Janice queried.

Emma then said, "Well, about two hundred or close to that. I know I have told well over one hundred." (Free advertising)

Janice continued listening to Emma recount the experience as Emma graphically conveyed the details, the hurt and the pain, with tears. It was cathartic. As Janice listened, she asked permission to ask her a question.

Emma said, "Sure, what is it?"

Janice repeated the number of people whom she had told and asked, "Would you be willing to tell one more person?"

"Who might that be?" Emma asked.

Janice said, "The administrator. She may not be aware of the pain you have experienced. In addition to the all the others who know about this, it might be beneficial for her to know that."

Emma gasped. She became very still and silent, as tears filled her eyes. Then she said, "I couldn't do that. She's an administrator. She's a nice person, and I don't want to stir up anything with her. And besides, it's been a long time ago, she probably doesn't remember it."

The two discussed the impact of the experience and the lingering effects and several possible approaches. Emma said she would like some time to think about it.

Two weeks later in a follow-up conversation, she stated firmly to Janice, "I'll get over it someday, but I'm not going to tell her." She didn't want Janice to speak to, confront, complain, or criticize the one person who might alter the pain of the situation.

A growth opportunity was missed for both individuals. This was a reckless hit-and-run. No call was made to report the incident, not the critizen, nor by any of the witnesses (those who comprised the critizone) who were present at the scene. The critic was following policy and procedure, oblivious that there had even been an event. So, the critizen was left alone with the after effects of the hit-and-run.

Criticism is rarely life threatening. It can be life altering in a negative or positive vein—even lifesaving. So except in life-threatening situations, prudence yields to the wisdom of an assessment of the criticism, taking into account the critizone, by the critic before presenting and by the critizen before responding to ensure the best outcome, working wonders moving toward resolution and harmony, avoiding or diminishing tension, confusion and misunderstanding between the parties involved whether it is at home, at work, with members of an organization, at school, in the community and nation, or even the United Nations. Since we know that tools and methods of assessment provide valuable information to aid in addressing problems in various realms of life, let's add assessment of criticism to the list of factors that enhance our relationships. This is akin to the emergency department staff making assessments of patients to assure the best possible outcome for the patient, their family and friends, the hospital, staff, and in some instances, the general public.

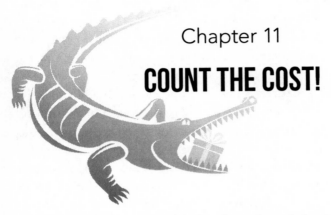

Chapter 11

COUNT THE COST!

Painful lessons learned the hard way from defensive, impulsive, default presentations and responses can pay huge benefit dividends for healing and maintaining healthy, vibrant relationships. It's a matter of counting the cost in advance by assessing situations and seeking mutually beneficial outcomes versus seeking to be right at the expense of the other being wrong. The cost savings in time and emotional energy can be profoundly significant, especially when compared to past experiences. Here's an example.

Prior to September 11, 2001, airline passengers needed two forms of ID (without a passport) for certain destinations. I drove my wife to the airport to assist with luggage and see her off on an international flight. After making all the necessary arrangements and provisions, we arrived at the airport for check-in, and upon being asked for two forms of ID, she realized she had only one form of ID in her purse. The airline representative was patient while Edwina presented her driver's license and searched for her voter registration card, to no avail.

Standing there observing the scene, I made an assessment of the situation (critizone). The line was backing up, the flight would be boarding soon, the agent wanted to check-in the others in line. It seemed that Edwina was embarrassed. I knew we would be riding back home together, so, I decided I wanted it to be a healing experience (mutually beneficial) to the degree it could be.

That's when I approached her and said, "What if we go home and get in touch with the voter registration office to get your card?"

She complied without any resistance. We had a pleasant ride home, discussing what actions either or both of us could take. Upon arriving home (prior to us having cell phones) the necessary phone calls were made, the voter registration card was obtained, and she made the next available flight.

Thankfully, I avoided compounding the situation by reminding her of what she should have done and other unhelpful criticisms. That would have added more hurt to her emotional injury. Instead, I provided the appropriate support, and there was nothing to apologize for (on this occasion).

Assessment helps make the most of the situation and realizes the greatest benefit when the widely-accepted belief that a situation is win or lose, reward or punishment, right or wrong, is suspended. The important thing is to enrich the human experience by enhancing the self-esteem of all parties rather than having one win while another loses—merely for the purpose of winning. Consider the question, "Is this the hill I want to die on?" (Translation—Is this the last thing I want to be known for)? This basic perspective can significantly alter what is done, yielding a more humane interaction. The shelf life may be a pleasant memory or teachable moment for all parties.

In essence, be neutral (objective) and be honest while assessing the critizone. Gather your emotions and establish control of yourself through diaphragmatic breathing and practice using role-play or the mirror as a means of developing various responses.

Like the broad array of team members in the emergency department, or the first responders on the scene of various situations, they are alert yet not panicked. Their mission and purpose is clear. They work quickly and are not harried. They work effectively in emergency situations, because they have trained extensively and gained knowledge, experience, and expertise to enhance their skills and control their emotions in the moment based on their level of responsibility and accountability in what would be a crisis to nearly everyone else. This is so because of the training, practice, rules, commitment, and the like.

Can you imagine emergency department personnel panicking at the sight of blood, burns, and broken limbs protruding through the flesh? Family members of loved ones and others may be in extreme panic mode; however, the emergency department staff is composed and professional, working to save lives and restore people to wholesome lives as best they can. We expect this of them. The patient's character, political affiliation, religious or academic standing, gender, or socioeconomic standing isn't supposed to affect the care the staff provides. (Insurance matters do play a role at times in these types of situations.) These professionals are always prepared, though not always aware of when or from where an impending emergency or crises situation will emerge. There are times when a physician, nurse, technician, social worker, EMT, or chaplain is called to the emergency room or other emergency situation from home, a party, or another function, or aroused from sleep. At times, he or she is faced with the reality of the death of a patient. Reckoning with the reality and finality of death is one aspect of their training. The training is frequent and often as opposed to occasional or seasonal, or when a survey or inspection is approaching. Additionally, the emergency department staff members are encouraged to practice self-care for their personal health and well-being.

Since most criticism isn't on an emergency level, before launching a criticism, *triage* the situation. Make an assessment to consider the vital aspects of the situation, gather your emotions, consider and develop options regarding presentation, weigh the likely responses, count the costs, and then act. Criticism need not be a life-and-death issue. It need not be the pretext for perpetual feuding. Instead and indeed, it could be a moment of discovery, healing, and growth for all parties. It could be a gift.

Imagine what it would be like if a member of the medical staff had only one impulsive response to you or any patient in an emergency situation. No triage, no medical assessment, no vital signs, no pulse, no look at the pupils, no blood pressure, no blood tests, no scans, only an impulsive reaction. He asks no questions of you or a loved one regarding medical history or allergies. The physician automatically administers a defibrillator shock to the patient because that's what he feels like doing in the moment. This has become part of his practice with all of the patients in the emergency department.

The absurdity of the example above is obvious. Of course, a medical team will take vital signs and gather essential information, triage the patient according to his or her condition, and consider the staffing levels and capabilities of the facility as part of the plan of action.

The triage method of ranking the patient's condition determines the appropriate response and level of care to provide valuable lessons in developing appropriate ways of offering and responding to criticism rather than acting solely on impulse or emotions. The likely outcome will be to improve relationships, lower costs (social, physical, emotional, financial, free advertising), lower and sometimes remove the barriers of win/lose, lying, denial, ego and pride, and enhance the experience.

There are times when criticism may lead to a loss. It could be a job, promotion, demotion, separation, divorce, a child leaving home, or the loss of another special relationship. These types of situations can be faced with minimal volatility. For ideas about a variety of approaches to life situations, refer to the book *Life Scripts* by Stephen M. Pollen and Mark Levine. You will find interesting ways of presenting and responding to situations at work or home and in the community, with multiple options.

Sometimes a loss can lead to a healing experience, presenting opportunities to grow that may have otherwise been obviated, ignored, or denied. There is a saying that can be applied in times like these:

> What happened isn't the most important thing—how we respond to what happened matters more.
>
> —Unknown

Whistleblowers sometimes suffer loss for being responsible and displaying the courage to report on matters of fraud, corruption, or danger to coworkers or the public at large. They complain and criticize. They may count the cost, act in good faith, and still pay a huge price with clear consciences. Their courage and suffering can bring change that reveals wrongdoing and provides correction and some protection to those who are innocent. And the whistleblower may be punished for daring to complain or criticize. For an eye-opening, sobering, focused book on whistleblowers and beyond, I recommend *Willful Blindness* by Margaret Heffernan.

Be judicious—be courageous!

There is a cost for acting or for not acting. Beware!

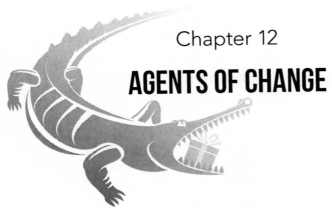

Chapter 12

AGENTS OF CHANGE

The current world we live in today—did not exist—once upon a time. It has come to be through change agents who dreamed or thought of something different; then set about making the changes. Ideas, thoughts, problems and questions emerge seeking hosts who dedicate and commit themselves to the vision. Stretching the mind, stirring curiosity, enduring sacrifice, ignoring discomfort, daring creativity are factors that join forces and brings into existence that which was once a dream and is revealed before us today. Individuals, families, groups and organizations dedicate and commit themselves to bring ideas to fruition, or leave a legacy upon which others can build.

Listed below are the names of a mere few individuals who were presented with specific ideas or problems that challenged themselves and others. They nonetheless probed, pursued, examined, explored, discovered and implemented their place in history and even into our lives today. After reading or perusing this brief list perhaps you will consider joining me and others to contribute to a new way of presenting and responding to criticism that will have mutually beneficial outcomes. The idea of living in harmony may be as daunting as any listed below, and yet can still be pursued and achieved.

- Wilbur and Orville Wright developed the first successful airplane in Kitty Hawk, North Carolina—and together they became national heroes. Considered the fathers of modern aviation, they developed innovative technology and inspired imaginations around the world.

- George Washington Carver is known for his work with peanuts (though he did not invent peanut butter, as some may believe). However, there's a lot more to this scientist and inventor than simply being the "Peanut Man." He was known as the young "plant doctor." In 1920, Carver spoke at the United Peanut Association of America's convention. He was such a success that the group decided to have him tell Congress about peanuts and the need for a tariff in January of 1921.

- Frederick Douglass was a prominent American abolitionist, author, and orator. Born a slave, Douglass escaped at age twenty and went on to become a world-renowned antislavery activist. His three autobiographies are considered important works of the slave narrative tradition as well as classics of American autobiography. Douglass's work as a reformer ranged from his abolitionist activities in the early 1840s to his attacks on Jim Crow and lynching in the 1890s. As a stalwart Republican, Douglass was appointed marshal (1877–1881) and recorder of deeds (1881–1886) for the District of Columbia, and *chargé d'affaires* for Santo Domingo and minister to Haiti (1889–1891).

- Ignaz Semmelweis (July 1, 1818–August 13, 1865), also Ignác Semmelweis (born Semmelweis Ignác Fülöp), was a Hungarian physician called the "savior of mothers" who discovered, by 1847, that the incidence of puerperal fever, also known as childbed fever, could be drastically cut by the use of handwashing standards in obstetrical clinics. Semmelweis introduced handwashing with chlorinated lime solutions for interns who had performed autopsies. This immediately reduced the incidence of fatal puerperal fever from about 10 percent (range 5–30 percent) to about 1–2 percent. At the time, diseases were attributed to many different and unrelated causes. Each case was considered unique, just like a human person is unique.

   Semmelweis's hypothesis, that there was only one cause, that all that mattered was cleanliness, was extreme at the time, and was largely ignored, rejected, or ridiculed. He was dismissed from the hospital and harassed by the medical community in Vienna, which eventually forced him to move to Budapest.

   Semmelweis was outraged by the indifference of the medical profession and began writing open and increasingly angry letters to prominent European obstetricians, at times denouncing them as irresponsible murderers. His contemporaries, including his wife, believed he was losing his mind, and he was committed to an asylum (mental institution) in 1865. Semmelweis died there only fourteen days later, possibly after being severely beaten by guards.

Semmelweis's practice only earned widespread acceptance years after his death, when Louis Pasteur developed the germ theory of disease that offered a theoretical explanation for Semmelweis's findings. Semmelweis is considered a pioneer of antiseptic procedures.

The Semmelweis reflex or "Semmelweis effect" is a metaphor for the reflex-like tendency to reject new evidence or new knowledge because it contradicts established norms, beliefs, or paradigms.

- Fannie Lou Hamer was a civil rights activist who helped African Americans register to vote and who cofounded the Mississippi Freedom Democratic Party.

In 1962, she met civil rights activists who encouraged blacks to register to vote, and soon became active in helping. Hamer also worked for the Student Nonviolent Coordinating Committee, which fought racial segregation and injustice in the South. In 1964, she helped found the Mississippi Freedom Democratic Party.

When young civil rights workers arrived in Ruleville in the Mississippi Delta in 1962, they were looking for local black people who could help convince their neighbors to register to vote. They found forty-four-year-old Fannie Lou Hamer.

Hamer was attracted to the young people, especially those in the Student Nonviolent Coordinating Committee (SNCC). "They treated us like we were special, and we loved 'em," she said. "We trusted 'em." For the rest of her life, Hamer would work in the civil rights movement on both the state and national stage. She felt that civil rights was her calling, her mission: "One day I know the struggle will change. There's got to be a change—not only for Mississippi, not only for the people in the United States, but people all over the world."

Many people first heard the phrase "I'm sick and tired of being sick and tired" from Fannie Lou Hamer.

- While working as an engineer for the Edison Illuminating Company in Detroit, Henry Ford (1863–1947) built his first gasoline-powered horseless carriage, the Quadricycle, in the shed behind his home. In 1903, he established the Ford Motor Company, and five years later the company rolled out the first Model T. In order to meet overwhelming demand for the revolutionary vehicle, Ford introduced revolutionary new mass-production methods, including large production plants, the use of standardized, interchangeable parts and, in 1913, the world's first moving assembly line for cars.

The rest is history.

- Dr. Martin Luther King Jr. was a Baptist minister and social activist, who led the Civil Rights Movement in the United States from the mid-1950s until his death by assassination in 1968. Martin Luther King Jr. was born on January 15, 1929, in Atlanta, Georgia. King, a Baptist minister and civil rights activist, had a seismic impact on race relations in the United States, beginning in the mid-1950s. Among his many efforts, King headed the Southern Christian Leadership Conference. Through his activism and inspirational speeches, he played a pivotal role in ending the legal segregation of African American citizens in the United States, as well as the creation of the Civil Rights Act of 1964 and the Voting Rights Act of 1965. King received the Nobel Peace Prize in 1964, among several other honors. He was assassinated in April 1968, and continues to be remembered as one of the most influential and inspirational African American leaders in history.

- Dr. Dorothy Height was born in Richmond, Virginia, on March 24, 1912. She was the daughter of James Edward Height, a building contractor, and Fannie Burroughs Height, a nurse. When Dorothy Height was very young, the family moved to Rankin, Pennsylvania, not far from Pittsburgh, where she attended integrated schools. Although she taught Bible stories to white children at her church, she was hurt at the age of nine when her best friend, a white girl, told her that she could not play with her any longer because Height was black.

As a high school student, Height made a speech about slavery amendments to the US Constitution that won her a scholarship to the college of her choice. Although she was accepted at Barnard College in New York City, when she showed up to enroll there, she was told the college's quota for blacks had been filled. Instead, she enrolled in New York University, where she earned a bachelor's degree in social sciences and a master's degree in educational psychology.

As a young woman, Height made time to join church-sponsored and civic groups. She continued her voluntary service in these organizations even after she graduated from New York University in 1932.

Height caught the attention of U.S. government leaders and human rights activists as a representative to international Young Women's Christian Association (YWCA) meetings. In 1966, she served on the council to the White House conference "To Fulfill These Rights." Height also worked with Delta Sigma Theta sorority, serving as its national president from 1946 to 1957. She never married.

By the 1960s, Height was at the forefront of the civil rights movement. She worked closely with the movement's major leaders, including King, Roy Wilkins, Whitney Young, and A. Philip Randolph, and she participated in nearly all of the major civil and human rights events of the era.

In 1964, Height initiated the National Council of Negro Women's "Wednesdays in Mississippi" program, in which women activists from the North flew south to spend Wednesdays in small towns, meeting with black women. One such meeting, held in a church in Hattiesburg, Mississippi, was nearly the scene of tragedy after someone threw a Molotov cocktail through the church window. Fortunately, the bomb did not ignite.

During Height's years as a civil rights activist, she never acquired a reputation as a radical or militant. Height received little attention for her work, perhaps because the movement was dominated by men. But Height told *People* in 1998, "If you worry about who is going to get credit, you don't get much work done." James Farmer, a former leader of the Congress for Racial Equality, credited Height with bringing the women's movement into the civil rights struggle.

- Marie Curie, *née* Maria Sklodowska, was born in Warsaw on November 7, 1867, the daughter of a secondary-school teacher. She received a general education in local schools and some scientific training from her father. She became involved in a students' revolutionary organization and found it prudent to leave Warsaw, then in the part of Poland dominated by Russia, for Cracow, which at that time was under Austrian rule. In 1891, she went to Paris to continue her studies at the Sorbonne where she obtained licentiateships in physics and the mathematical sciences. She met Pierre Curie, professor in the school of physics in 1894, and in the following year they were married. She succeeded her husband as head of the physics laboratory at the Sorbonne, gained her doctor of science degree in 1903, and following the tragic death of Pierre Curie in 1906, she took his place as professor of general physics in the faculty of sciences, the first time a woman had held this position. She was also appointed director of the Curie Laboratory in the Radium Institute of the University of Paris, founded in 1914.

Her early researches, together with her husband, were often performed under difficult conditions, laboratory arrangements were poor and both had to undertake much teaching to earn a livelihood. The discovery of radioactivity by Henri Becquerel in 1896 inspired the Curies in their brilliant researches and analyses which led to the isolation of polonium, named after the country of Marie's birth, and radium. Mme. Curie developed methods for the separation of radium from radioactive residues in sufficient quantities to allow for its characterization and the careful study of its properties, therapeutic properties in particular.

She retained her enthusiasm for science throughout her life and did much to establish a radioactivity laboratory in her native city. In 1929 President Hoover of the United States presented her with a gift of $50,000, donated by American friends of science, to purchase radium for use in the laboratory in Warsaw. Mme. Curie, quiet, dignified, and unassuming, was held in high esteem and admiration by scientists throughout the world. She was a member of the Conseil du Physique Solvay from 1911 until her death and since 1922 she had been a member of the Committee of Intellectual Cooperation of the League of Nations.

The importance of Mme. Curie's work is reflected in the numerous awards bestowed on her. She received many honorary science, medicine and law degrees and honorary memberships of learned societies throughout the world. Together with her husband, she was awarded half of the Nobel Prize for physics in

1903, for their study into the spontaneous radiation discovered by Becquerel, who was awarded the other half of the prize. In1911 she received a second Nobel Prize, this time in chemistry, in recognition of her work in radioactivity. She also received, jointly with her husband, the Davy Medal of the Royal Society in 1903 and, in 1921, President Harding of the United States, on behalf of the women of America, presented her with one gram of radium in recognition of her service to science.

- On May 6 in 1954, at the Iffley Road Track in Oxford, England, medical student Roger Bannister became the first person in recorded history to run the mile in under four minutes.

Roger Bannister was born in Middlesex on March 23, 1929. His parents couldn't afford to send him to school, so he ran his way in: Bannister won a track scholarship to Oxford, where he studied medicine and was a running sensation. He caused a furor in England when he declined to run the fifteen-hundred meters in the 1948 London Olympics so he could concentrate on his medical studies. He did run in the 1952 Olympics in Helsinki, but finished fourth. Again, the British press scorned him. He then resolved to break track and field's most famous barrier, the four-minute mile, a feat many believed to be impossible. Bannister had limited time to train, as he was enrolled at St. Mary's Hospital Medical School. He would run thirty minutes most days, focusing the rest of his time on his study of neurology.

On May 6, 1954, Bannister was running for the Amateur Athletic Association in Oxford against runners from the university in their annual match. He ran with two friends, who paced him, and then sprinted the last two hundred yards, for a record time of 3:59.4. Later that month, Australian John Landy broke Bannister's record by less than a second. The two were then made out to be rivals.

- Civil rights activist Rosa Parks refused to surrender her bus seat to a white passenger, spurring the Montgomery boycott and other efforts to end segregation.

Civil rights activist Rosa Parks was born on February 4, 1913, in Tuskegee, Alabama. Her refusal to surrender her seat to a white passenger on a Montgomery, Alabama bus spurred a citywide boycott. The city of Montgomery had no choice but to lift the law requiring segregation on public buses and helped launch nationwide efforts to end segregation of public facilities.

Rosa Parks received many accolades during her lifetime, including the National Association for the Advancement of Colored People's highest award.

- Septima Poinsette Clark was a teacher and civil rights activist whose citizenship schools helped enfranchise and empower African Americans. Born on May 3, 1898, in Charleston, South Carolina, Septima Poinsette Clark branched out into social action with the NAACP while working as a teacher. As part of the Southern Christian Leadership Conference, she set up citizenship schools that helped many African Americans register to vote.

  In 1961, the Southern Christian Leadership Conference (SCLC) took over this education project. Clark then joined the SCLC. She retired from the SCLC in 1970. In 1979, Jimmy Carter honored her with a Living Legacy Award. She received the Order of the Palmetto, South Carolina's highest civilian honor, in 1982. Clark was eighty-nine when she died on December 15, 1987, on South Carolina's Johns Island.

These few among myriad other agents of change helped transform society and the world. They were aided by a host of others who supported, coached, taught, mentored, challenged, and at times criticized each other. They faced major obstacles in many realms and yet remained steadfast to their calling. They were driven or compelled to bring about change, refusing to settle for the status quo, never being complacent, never giving up—even in the face of intense opposition. Some were drafted into action. The opposition and resistance that accompanies change can be a pathway to growth, illustrating the principle that says:

A problem is an opportunity misunderstood.

New Frontiers

The idea of criticism as a gift may seem impossible. While I submit it's a challenge, it is no more so than any of the challenges presented earlier. For criticism to be a gift, three essential elements are necessary—concept, attitude, and practice—to bring about this change.

First, suspend the very common, almost universal win-lose,

right-wrong, fight-or-flight mentality, based on a survivalist mind-set that is ultimately dangerous, harmful, or destructive to relationships. This begins with checking emotions; having the brain stem confer with the frontal and temporal lobes to examine and question perceived threats; and seek insight and understanding to explore options of living and acting beyond competition. Examine, explore, question, and challenge the status quo and inherited presuppositions regarding criticism and relationships in general. Consider the possibility of harmony and mutually beneficial outcomes.

Second, view everyone as copartners (cooperating rather than competing) in the experience of life with a vast array of people we don't know and will never meet.

Some examples are the following:

- The growth and delivery of the food we eat—Other people, locally, nationally, and internationally, plant, cultivate, harvest, package, and transport the food we eat and enjoy to the local market or store. This happens on a daily basis. Is there a moment or thought of expressing appreciation or thanks for these unnamed, unknown partners?
- Transportation and travel—The roads, bridges, tunnels, airways, and oceans we traverse with faith and certain presuppositions are designed, built, managed, maintained, and cleared of snow, ice, and debris by people we will never meet. This is a major factor in our day-to-day lives for commerce, goods and services managed, supported and implemented by those who are unseen partners in a joint venture with other unseen partners. Give a word or thought of gratitude for them and the sacrifices they make in order to support our lifestyle.
- Electricity—The power grid and all the people who work to keep it operational partner with others during storms or at other times to get the system back on line; and to maintain it in less taxing situations. At least once a day, when using something that requires electricity, take a moment to say thank you.
- Water and associated utilities. Aqueducts, reservoirs, towers, and dams in countries around the world supply water to cities. Thank someone.
- Sewage treatment and associated utilities.

- Fuel refined and delivered to local stations or depots. Be glad for all the helpers.
- Medical supplies and equipment. Acknowledge the work of others.
- Internet purchases. Be grateful—even when the speed is slow.
- The raw materials used in manufacturing all the items that are almost taken for granted every day in the lives of many people, come from many other countries, extracted by people who may be regarded by some as less than human. The book *Less Than Human: Why We Demean, Enslave, and Exterminate Others* by David Livingstone Smith speaks to this topic. Support humane treatment for all those unnamed and exploited people.

I realize there are those who have no interest in partnering with others to make life more wholesome for all. Nonetheless, these individuals experience the results of partnership perhaps without consideration thereof. It is clear that we need and depend on each other, whether in cooperative or noncooperative ways.

We can work wonderfully well together on projects and other assignments that are associated with a job and a paycheck for an individual, family, community, corporation, or nation. Beyond the scope of the job or project some of the same individuals may ignore those they worked with earlier in the day. It could be at a restaurant, store, at the mall, or on the street: walk by and not speak or engage in any manner. And then the next day at work, life returns to the cycle of social or political correctness. Nothing is said about having seen anyone at the mall.

It seems clear that the masses are content to refuse to think, let alone believe, that we can live in harmony with each other beyond the boundaries of a job, volunteer assignment, paycheck or other experience with personal benefits. This in the face of apparently not knowing, recognizing or caring about our unavoidable interdependency.

If this is where you are in thought and belief, please review the chapter on the four stages of learning and contemplate what it might be like to learn more about others, move out of the comfort zone, and evolve though the awkwardness of learning to associate with others and move in the direction of harmony. Otherwise, we can be assured of the continuation of more competitive, divisive orders of the day that we have on the social, political, financial, religious, economic, and cultural fronts.

Consider how well the diverse bodies we all live in function so similarly well for each of us. The systems and subsystems of our bodies cooperate and participate magnificently enabling and empowering us to live, grow, learn, create, design, and build. We can also interact externally with other people (or not) who live in bodies with similar systems and subsystems. Through upgrades in medicine, technology and the social sphere, organs from one body can be donated, and transplanted to another; blood and blood products, tissue, and other elements can be shared from one person with a family member or with a complete stranger. This can happen beyond the boundaries of ethnicity, color, class, culture, socioeconomics, zip codes, and political or religious categories. Truly amazing! Often lifesaving and enriching!

Yet, when it comes to cooperation and harmony on a massive sustainable scale beyond the boundaries of ethnicity, color, class, culture, socioeconomics, zip codes, politics, or religion, walls go up. There is retreat to the default inherited customs and practices. Lines are drawn in the sand. Barriers are erected, bolstered by fear, threats, and intimidation in the name of some type of purity, or preservation, to avoid change, to prevent one group from being contaminated by another. And so, it goes on and on.

Upgrade

I propose shifting to a paradigm of relationships being our greatest treasure, with an intent to build, establish, and maintain mutually beneficial relationships. Regarding everyone as copartners in the experience of life, linked with continued honing of vital communication skills—especially listening—will guide us in the direction of experiencing and believing that we can live in harmony and having mutually beneficial goals and outcomes in life for life.

Are you open to practicing, thinking, and believing along this path to actually see, hear, and feel the difference? This calls for a paradigm shift that begins with each individual and multiplies exponentially.

A paradigm shift is a change from one way of thinking and acting to another. It's a sort of metamorphosis that is driven by agents of change. It doesn't "just happen."

The term *paradigm shift* was fathered, defined, and popularized in 1962 by Thomas Kuhn in his work *The Structure of Scientific Revolutions*. He states that scientific advancement is not evolutionary, but rather is a "series of peaceful interludes punctuated by intellectually violent revolutions," and in those revolutions "one conceptual world view is replaced by another."

Kuhn points to paradigm shifts ranging from the scientific theory of the Ptolemaic system (the earth at the center of the universe) to the Copernican system (the sun at the center of the universe); and from Newtonian physics to relativity and quantum physics. Each movement changed the worldview and, consequentially, the operations and functions of our lives. Former beliefs were replaced by the new paradigms creating "a new gestalt."

My reference to paradigm shifts in the social, scientific, and political arenas that altered the course of human events in this country and the larger world are cited as examples or illustrations of what has been done in very complex arenas that are now commonplace. Based on the facts of these changes, I am willing to believe that positive paradigm shifts can happen in the complex arenas of culture, social, class, language, community, and family. There is evidence, proof, stories, books, and movies of such experiences with a variety of individuals, couples, families, and groups that can be substantiated.

Yet I often receive staunch opposition to the notion that we can live in harmony, from people who say I'm living in a dream world, it'll never happen, or it can't happen. Rarely is there any interest or consideration of a demonstration of how this might work. The potential is dismissed, written off as a waste, with an invitation for me to get on with living in the real world. And yet, things that were once upon a time considered a dream, fantasy, passing fad, or impossible are fully embraced as if there was no struggle, opposition, or changes that accompanied the development of these things.

Even before the term paradigm shift was voiced, developed, or popularized, such shifts occurred throughout history, and will continue to occur.

Some of these include the following:

- The change from hunting and gathering to an agricultural-based society altered the landscape of many nations into small villages, each surrounded by patchy fields of corn, vegetables, and other foods that were planted, tended, and harvested manually. Then there was the shift to a mechanized means of food production. Today, this essential element of life (food) comes to us via mass-production planting, growing, harvesting, transporting, selling, and preparation, including GMOs (genetically modified organisms). These changes have given rise to an organic movement. These shifts occurred through various phases of design, experimentation, modification, resistance, implementation, and varying degrees of rejection, acceptance, and gratitude.

- The printing press changed cultures around the world and had a direct impact and dynamic effect on the scientific revolution. Gutenberg's invention of movable type in the 1440s was a quantum agent of change, making books readily available, smaller, and easier to handle as well as purchase.

- The world of communications and dissemination of information, as well as disinformation, has been drastically altered by the shifts from etchings, drums, and smoke signals to the telegraph to the telephone to radio and television. With the invention of the transistor and microchips, even more dramatic changes occurred to move industry from vacuum tubes, relays, switches and switchboards to computers, microprocessors, handheld devices, and the internet. Agents of change are driving new paradigm shifts in numerous realms today and every day. Paradigm shifts will be occurring forever. With fiber optics and nanotechnology, we may be approaching the introduction of GMP—genetically modified people. Some of you may be familiar with the term *transhuman*. Merely not knowing or not believing won't stop it.

- Shifts in transportation and travel have "made the world smaller." Advancements in tires roll us along great distances at varying speeds, in all kinds of weather, with large and small vehicles, bicycles, and motorcycles; tires enable airplanes to take off and land safely. By the way, tire companies are constantly "reinventing" the wheel.

- Social movements, such as women's suffrage, right to life, labor, human and civil rights, had major impacts on individuals, groups of people and nations that enhanced lives and offered rays of hope to those who for eons had been locked in dark cycles of despair. Courageous individuals, groups, activists, reporters, and camera crews, along with many who were poor, some wealthy, people with limited formal education alongside many learned individuals, opened windows and doors that shed light on some of the darker elements of those who held others in their grip of bondage with utterly inhuman treatment. This shift enabled and empowered

3

masses of liberated people to begin exploring new ways of living and being.

- Third, this book is a call for a paradigm shift across the spectrum of society related to the universal experience of criticism. The impact of unskilled criticism typically leads to strong emotional responses and reactions often manifested in intense stress, anger, hurt, disappointment, devaluing, retaliation, or revenge. This book provides information and presents skills that can reduce stress, tension, and friction, and defuse or diffuse potentially explosive situations, resulting in mutually beneficial understanding and consideration of harmony.

Improvements in this universal area begin with a paradigm shift to enhance our communication criticism skills up to twenty-first-century standards. It is possible, in many instances, if not most, to transform the negative aspects of criticism into positive outcomes for all parties, making it plausible to move from conflict and contest to conversation. To dance rather than fight as addressed in the chapter on communication skills.

In order to treasure relationships, they must be more than competitive events. It is important to distinguish between the people in the events of life and not limit or equate the people in the games of life with the games. Take the people off the field, track, court, and floor, and out of the competitive arena and into our arms, hearts, and lives to the extent and degree that is feasible and practical.

Family life is at the core of our lives and society. No matter the format, everyone comes from a family—at least to this point in time.

In the book, *Why Marriages Succeed or Fail*, Dr. John Gottman, a psychologist at the University of Washington in Seattle, identifies three styles of marriage relationships as affirming, adversarial, and avoidant. These identified styles have application to relationships at work, politics, economics, athletics, community, and social life as well as criticism. Dr. Gottman is quoted in an article in the SixWise newsletter dated April 8, 2013, saying, "Working briefly on your marriage (relationship) every day will do more for your health and longevity than working out at a health club." In the same newsletter, relationships are listed as the number one stressor in today's world. According to Pat Swan, MS, CMFT, a marriage and family therapist,

> More than 90 percent of my clients suffering from depression, anxiety or other mental illnesses have one primary complaint—relationship problems at work or at home.

Typically, those in close relationships at work, social situations, home, and community are wary of expressing criticism due to fear of being misunderstood, hurting feelings, losing relationships, or causing reprisal or retribution. Keeping silent and avoiding the presentation of meaningful observations, helpful thoughts, or feelings may become a breeding ground for tension, frustration, and slow and steady erosion of former wholesome relationships. Responding in an explosive manner or silently seething may likewise yield harmful outcomes. The cumulative effect of avoiding and ignoring critical matters can result in damaged or disruptive situations, outbursts, withdrawal, violence, death, and even war. The aftermath involves the high costs of clean up, working to repair and rebuild all that was destroyed; support the lives of grieving family members, loved ones, colleagues, and friends of those who died or were killed; mend relationships, job, careers, communities, and nations. These calamities may have been avoided if the skills that were used after the fight, after the damage, after the arrest, after the funeral, after the war had been employed much earlier. After the carnage, we come to resolution and agreements. Afterward we talk, listen, clarify, apologize, make amends, and in some instances, pay reparations. Afterward, we become trading partners. The skills used after the turmoil can be effective before beginning the turmoil and yield the likelihood that fighting becomes unnecessary.

Imagine your world and beyond evolving into a more tranquil place to live, work, play, study, meditate, travel, reflect, share and enjoy to the utmost! I refer to this possibility as Relationships 2.0, made possible through Communication 2.0 which includes Criticism 2.0

Maintaining a positive attitude supported by skills is part of life's ongoing work that keeps paying rich dividends, even on off days when you may not be at your best. Having options in the ways we communicate and relate provides a defined benefit over the impulsive attack-defend, right-wrong, win-lose attitude and behavior.

We can live in harmony!

Chapter 13

THE BIGGEST ROOM IN THE WORLD

I encourage us to make ourselves uncomfortable and learn new ways of responding to and presenting criticism. Proficiency in this area will have far-reaching impact on the lives of those with whom we have contact and on our own selves. We will see, hear, and feel the difference as we alter, adapt, adjust, and become skilled in presenting and responding to criticism. In so doing, this practice can reach a tipping point and become viral, reshaping the landscape of those in your sphere and beyond toward greater harmony and maturity.

An incentive to aid and promote the practice of making yourself uncomfortable in the realm of criticism, is to do something different intentionally in other areas of your life on a consistent basis. Changes in one area of experience can prompt changes in other areas of life, including the manner of our communication and criticism. The science of neuroplasticity has updated our understanding and beliefs about the changeability of the brain. Those who are willing can explore beyond the inherited and former beliefs and teachings, reach and stretch to new horizons.

Some suggestions for doing things differently include the following:

- Fold your arms across your chest and notice which arm is on top. Now put the other arm on top. Many people report feeling awkward initially. As you continue putting the other arm on top, you will adjust and feel comfortable with the different configuration.
- Clasp your hands together noticing which thumb is on top. Now clasp your hands with the other thumb on top. Feel the difference? Practice until you become comfortable with either thumb on top.

- Take a different route to work or home. Plan appropriately for needed adjustments with the time factor and, if warranted, inform the appropriate parties of the changes in your routine.
- If you jump rope for exercise, note the foot you start off on with the single leg jumps. Now begin your routine by pushing off on the other foot.
- Learn to swim.
- If you swim, and breathe only on one side, alter your workout by breathing on the other side.
- Cyclists, note which foot you push off with at the start of your ride and which foot you put down first when you stop. Now alter the foot you push off and stop with. If you use clipless pedals, be all the more attentive and careful, especially as you unlock and prepare to stop. You might also prepare yourself for a fall or two.
- Which hand do you typically write with? Which hand do you use to feed yourself? What is your hand configuration as you shovel snow? Now alter that which is typical and do the opposite.
- Occasionally read upside down.
- Do some math without a calculator.
- Eat with chop sticks.
- Learn a new language. Take classes. Learn from a friend. Use Pimsleur, Rosetta Stone, or other resources.
- Play a new instrument or refresh your former musical skills.
- Play in a different key.
- Improve your eating habits.
- Chew your food longer.
- Start an exercise program, or enhance your exercise program. (Check with a professional to ensure a program that will be right for you.)
- Refresh yourself with various activities that have found their way onto the "used-to-do" list.
- For the bold of heart and spirit, periodically alter the presentation of yourself in specific contexts. Laugh more, smile more, smile less, and keep silent for longer periods of time, or speak up.
- Teachers familiar with "wait time" or "think time" can attest to the positive benefits of silence between questions and responses in the classroom. The concept of wait time as an instructional variable was invented by Mary Budd Rowe (1972). The (wait-time)

periods of silence that followed teacher questions and students completed responses rarely lasted more than 1.5 seconds in typical classrooms. She discovered, however, that when these periods of silence lasted at least three seconds, many positive things happened to students' and teachers' behaviors and attitudes. Learning to wait in periods of silence can be awkward. Breathe and listen.

- Talk less.
- Turn off the TV or radio. Ride in your car in silence occasionally.
- Tie your necktie on the other side of your collar.
- Put your contacts in with the other hand.
- Teach children to tell time using an analog clock.

Discovery is the bonus!

Awkwardness will likely accompany these modifications, proving that you are changing.

Intentionally, on purpose in various ways, make yourself uncomfortable to boost your brain power and problem-solving abilities, including communication, relationship, and criticism abilities. There is an abundance of material on brain neuroplasticity encouraging us to take on new experiences beyond the realm of age, socioeconomic status, health status, or other acculturated or imposed boundaries and beliefs.

Bear in mind the impact that innovators make on the world by moving out of their comfort zones, expanding horizons, discovering, sacrificing, creating, and inventing. The world we live in today is part of our inheritance and will be modified by those who see beyond. This is a vital element in changing the world whether in small or significant ways. From candles to electric lights; writing to typewriters to computers to iPads; mimeograph machines to copiers to 3D printers; analog to digital; smoke signals to the telegraph to the telephone to cell phones to computers to the internet, to gene editing - these and other changes went through near perpetual experimentation, error, updates, and modifications to bring the ideas into existence.

The only way to avoid the discomfort of change is to remain the same, refuse to change, refuse to grow, and perpetually abide in the present state. Put the Do Not Disturb sign on the door of your life's potential to let others know to leave you alone and just go away. Keep in mind that even with those who vehemently resist change in outlook, perspective, attitude, and behavior, their bodies continually change in order to keep them alive. Even death cannot stop changes from occurring in the body.

Reasons and excuses for not changing abound to the point of filling warehouses and becoming virtual—accompanying people along the course of their journey. Providing a degree of comfort for remaining in the status quo.

The option of discovery and exploration calls for change that will be awkward, with some degree of discomfort.

When I want to enhance my ability and skill in playing the piano, I find a teacher who plays at least seven levels beyond my abilities. I am prepared to seek, welcome, and receive criticism as part of the learning experience. Furthermore, I expect the teacher to critique or criticize my efforts.

I would expect similar feedback or critique if I were learning a new language, martial arts, flying lessons, plumbing, or a plethora of other things in life. Errors and mistakes can be regarded as indicators of learning, growing, improving, and progressing. After all, the biggest room in the world is the room for improvement.

Based on my work, observations, experience, and desire to live in harmony, I have reframed the notion of criticism as being "negative," as being something bad or necessarily wrong, to a reference point or a baseline indicator of where one is in a specific context. I can apply this to, for instance, electricity, which has a negative and a positive pole. Batteries have a positive and a negative terminal, and in order for electricity to flow, both poles or terminals are required, and there is a connection between them. Neither is bad or wrong.

The terminals or poles are reference points. This applies in other areas of life. When I want to play jazz chords in different keys there are the two terminals, a beginning and a destination. Negative is where I am in my ability to play in the keys of C and G. As I practice and perform. my playing moves in the positive direction to where I am going. Adding new keys to my skill set requires some awkwardness or negative feelings for a while. Negative is my ability to play initially. Positive will become manifest as I practice and improve. As I become familiar and comfortable with all twelve keys, I can make myself uncomfortable and learn new styles of music. And the learning goes on and on.

Keep in mind: "negative" is a reference point, and "positive" is the direction of the desired destination. At most malls, there is a directory or map that shows the layout of the stores. There is a symbol or marker that says, "You are here." This is a reference point, where you are. Knowing where you are (negative) informs you of the direction and distance of the journey for where you want to go (positive). With this information, you can more easily and intentionally navigate and chart your course. Interestingly, your arrival at the current desired destination now becomes where you are (negative). And so, the journey goes on continually. This continual change of location allows for the continued pursuit of the many avenues of living.

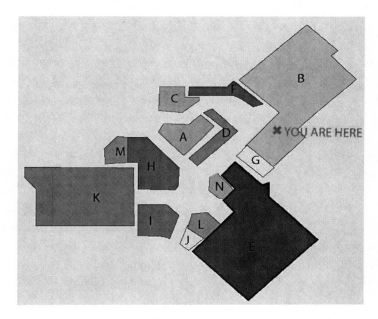

Arriving and remaining at a given point (negative) interminably would be a negative in light of all the room there is in the world. Perhaps that's the bad part of a negative experience. This ensures no progress, no flow of current in the direction of your desired destination or goal. This situation makes it more likely for this individual to be used by others who have defined goals.

Ignoring the criticism and balking at it may reveal a character flaw, a lack of ego strength, an overly ambitious goal, or other factors, including an unacknowledged weakness, or an I-don't-care attitude. Becoming overly comfortable, confident, or fearful can lead to the disaster of complacency, ignoring, or denying crucial information, or satisfaction with the status quo in order to avoid the discomfort of learning and growing.

There are times when complacency can lead to ignoring or discounting information and warnings that can lead to disaster. Consider the reports of warnings related to the attacks on the World Trade Centers, as was the case with numerous warnings that were ignored or overlooked regarding the state of the levies in New Orleans prior to hurricanes Katrina and Rita. Could things have turned out differently had these warnings been seriously investigated? Some will say let's move on—what is done is done. Such attitudes are an example of blaming history and refusing to learn the lessons thereof, which means a repetition of a similar experience.

Dr. Andrew Lo of MIT proclaims that there were three major elements that led to the financial collapse of the housing market in the previous decade: 1) human nature [*I would say human behavior*]; 2) advanced technology; 3) the lack of negative feedback. What I gathered from his lecture is, had the revelations about misdeeds, greed, corruption, and crimes been taken seriously and acted upon or had there been more reports and revelations in higher places of power and influence, perhaps there would have been successful interventions that would have spared the nation and millions of people from financial losses on an order of magnitude not seen in decades. Had the financial debacle been averted, the lives of millions would have remained on track with their dreams, goals, and aspirations. As it has turned out, according to Dr. Lo, we are in this arena of uncertainty, turmoil, worry, and fear, headed toward who knows where, all because of a lack of courage to express negative feedback. Instead, greed and arrogance disguised as ignorance served as justification for the horrific losses and damage at the root of this tragedy.

You can yield, maintaining the status quo of comfort and convenience in all areas of life, or you can make yourself uncomfortable, acquaint yourself with risk, and proceed with your dreams, your life, and experience what others only dream of! Let's work together and enlarge the biggest room in the world.

I'd like to close this book with one song among many that helps keep me willing to search and explore beyond my comfort zone.

The song "The Higher You Climb" by Dan Fogelberg abides with me. The refrain is as follows:

> The higher you climb, the more that you see
> The more that you see, the less that you know
> The less that you know, the more you yearn
> The more you yearn, the higher you climb.

Mountaintop experiences are wonderful, grand, and glorious, giving a sense of accomplishment and achievement, perhaps a degree of pride, deserving of celebration and recognition.

After a while you look into the distance, and behold, there is another mountain, sometimes higher than the one you're presently on. The requirement for having the next mountaintop experience is to depart and go down through the valley that leads to the next mountain.

> Go ahead—Make yourself uncomfortable. Make your day and experience a fuller life.

> Criticism, like rain, should be gentle enough to nourish a man's growth without destroying his roots.
> —Frank A. Clark

Quotes

(Those without attribution are the author's)

To avoid criticism, say nothing, do nothing, be nothing.
—Aristotle

The biggest room in the world is the room for improvement!
—Unremembered

As we think in our hearts so are we (or) so we become.
—Proverbs 23:7

When you change the way you look at things,
the things you look at change.
—Dr. Wayne Dyer

Begin with the end in mind.
—Steven Covey

More than 90 percent of my clients suffering from depression,
anxiety or other mental illnesses have one primary
complaint—relationship problems at work or at home.
—Pat Swan

When in the course of human events it becomes necessary for one
people to dissolve the political bands which have connected them with
another and to assume among the powers of the earth, the separate
and equal station to which the Laws of Nature and of Nature's God
entitle them, a decent respect to the opinions of mankind requires
that they should declare the causes which impel them to separate.
—Thomas Jefferson

Poor communication is today's number one problem at work, at home and in the world at large. Discords among people are frequent, from small annoyances like twenty-minute phone mail messages, to lifelong parent-child resentments, to intractable conflicts between nations.
—Shelle Rose Charvet

Poor communication skills yield communication that kills.

Body language and other unconscious revelations are privileged information, to be treated as such.

If nothing ever changed there'd be no butterflies.
—Unknown

A problem is an opportunity misunderstood.
—Dr. Dale Hannah

Triage the situation, assess the significance, and act appropriately.

If you want to learn to love better, you should start with a friend who you hate.
—Johann Wolfgang von Goethe

Criticism, like rain, should be gentle enough to nourish a man's growth without destroying his roots.
—Frank A. Clark

When told I am dreaming, I keep on dreaming.

The first to present his case seems right, till another comes forward and questions him.
—Proverbs 18:17

When words are many, transgression is not lacking, but he who restrains his tongue is prudent.
—Proverbs 10:19

The more words, the more vanity, and how does that benefit anyone?
—Ecclesiastes 6:11 (modified)

Think about what you say.
—On marquee of the Holocaust Museum in Washington, DC

The person who criticizes me is doing me a favor that
many people would be very reluctant to do.

No one knows all there is to know about all there is to know.

No one gets out alive.

Laughter does good like a medicine.
—Proverbs 17:22 NIV

The more things you carry, the more you weigh.

The universe is filled with genies waiting to do your bidding.
—Unknown

I love you, and because I love you, I would sooner have you hate
me for telling you the truth than adore me for telling you lies.
—Pietro Aretino

Criticism and dissent are the indispensable antidote to major delusions.
—Alan Barth

Let the first impulse pass, wait for the second.
—Baltasar Gracian

What happened isn't the most important thing—how
we respond to what happened matters more.
—Unknown

If you can't win, make the one ahead of you break the record.
—Unknown

Open rebuke is better than hidden love.
—Proverbs 27:5 KJV

Denial is more than a river in Egypt.

—Unknown

Remember if perfection is your goal, you may well be chasing a mirage.

Make sure your worth far exceeds your wealth.

Ranking has a place in life, just not in the value of any person.

The potential of all is potentially in each,
uniquely expressed by the individual.

Imagination is more important than knowledge, for knowledge is limited
to all we now know and understand, while imagination embraces the
entire world, and all there ever will be to know and understand.

—Albert Einstein

The brain is the only container that has this unique feature.
The more you put into it, the more it will hold.

—Unknown

References/Bibliography

Adler, R. B., & J. M. Elmhorst. A brief outline of criticism entitled: Dealing with Criticism. Communication at Work—UNCG University Speaking Center. speakingcenter.uncg.edu. (1996)

Alexander, Noble. *I Will Die Free.*

Allport, Gordon. *Scale of Prejudice and Discrimination.* Harvard University, 1954.

Blakeslee, Matthew and Sandra Blakeslee. *The Body Has a Mind of Its Own.* New York: Random House, 2007.

Burrell, Tom. *Brainwashed.* New York: Smiley Books, 2010.

Charvet, Shelle Rose. *Words That Change Minds (Mastering the Language of Influence).* Dubuque, Iowa: Kendall/Hunt, 1997.

Covey, Steven. *The 7 Habits of Highly Effective People.* New York: Simon & Schuster, 2004.

Dawson, George, and Richard Glaubman. *Life Is So Good.* New York: Random House, 2000.

Dobson, Terry and Victor Miller. *Aikido in Everyday Life.* Berkeley: North Atlantic Books, 1993.

Ford, Debbie. *The Dark Side of the Light Chasers.* New York: Riverhead Books, 1998.

Gendlin, Eugene T. *Focusing.* New York: Bantam Books, 1981.

Gottman, John. *Why Marriages Succeed or Fail.* New York: Simon and Schuster, 1994.

Kohn, Alife. *No Contest.* New York: Houghton Mifflin Company, 1992.

Kuhn, Thomas. *The Structure of Scientific Revolutions.* University of Chicago Press, 1962.

Maisel, Eric. *Toxic Criticism.* New York: McGraw-Hill, 2007.

McGowan, Thomas G. "The Dangers of Violent Political Language." *The Commercial Appeal.* Online News Wire. Memphis, 2011

Holy Bible, New International Version. Nashville: Holman Bible Publishers, 1999.

Holy Bible, King James Version. Nashville: Thomas Nelson Publishers, 1984.

Patterson, Grenny, McMillan and Switzler. *Crucial Confrontations.* New York: McGraw-Hill, 2005

Pollen, Stephen M., and Mark Levine. *Life Scripts.* Indianapolis: Wiley Publishing, Inc, 1996.

PubMed.gov.

Rosenthal, M. Zachary, Melissa A. Polusny, and Victoria M. Follette, Victoria M. "Avoidance Mediates the Relationship Between Perceived Criticism in the Family of Origin and Psychological Distress in Adulthood." *Journal of Emotional Abuse* 6, no. 1 (2006): 87–102.

Sullivan, Andrea. *A Path to Healing.* New York: Broadway Books, 1998.

Sixwise.com. "The Top Six Stressor Areas in Life: How to Recognize and Hand the Stress." SixWise Newsletter. April 8, 2013.

Slywotzky, Adrian J. *DEMAND.* New York: Crown Business, 2011.

Smith, David Livingstone. *Less Than Human: Why We Demean, Enslave, and Exterminate Others.* New York: St. Martin's Press, 2011.

Wadley, Jared. "Fighting Words: Violent Political Rhetoric Fuels Violent Attitudes." News Service, week of January 31, 2011.

Walker, Hezekiah. "I Need You to Sur⌐

Watterson, Kathryn. *Not by the Sw⌐*

Weisinger, Hendrie. *The Positive Powe⌐*
    1999.

Survey on Criticism

Getting Along Better, LLC—Relationship Consulting
Check all that apply. Comments are welcome. No names please.

What is your typical reaction to the word *criticism*?
___ Negative ___Optimistic ___Potentially helpful

Can criticism be helpful?
____Y ____N

Have you ever taken a class, workshop, seminar, or read a book on criticism?
____Y ____N

Have you ever benefitted from a criticism?
____Y ____N

Have you ever denied or ignored a criticism only to regret doing so?
____Y ____N

How do you tend to respond to criticism in general?
___ Avoid ___Embrace ___ Accept ___Deny
___Ignore ___Get even ___Anger ___Listen to learn

How do you tend to present criticism?
___ Reluctantly ___Regretfully ___Thoughtfully ___Optimistically

Are you likely to avoid giving a criticism—even when it is warranted?
___ Y ___ N

Would you do any of the following to enhance your presentation of or response to criticism?
____ Attend a seminar, workshop, webinar
____ Read a book on the topic

What prompts you to buy gasoline for your vehicle?
___The low gas signal ___1/4 tank ___1/2 tank

How do you respond to your body when it presents a criticism (i.e., headache, pain, indigestion, insomnia, thirst, anxiety)? __Ignore __Attend-record-act accordingly __Take a pill __Other __. Explain_____

Socioographics: __ Female __ Male __ Age __ Single __ Married __ Widowed __ Divorced __ Student __ Ethnicity Occupation_____

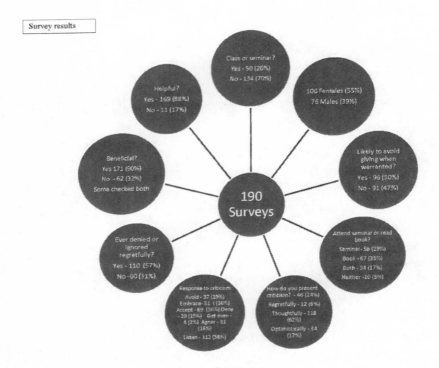

Revised 8.21.14

Index

CPSIA information can be obtained
at www.ICGtesting.com
Printed in the USA
FSOW01n1605280717
36887FS